PRESENTED TO:

_____

PET'S NAME

_____

OWNER'S NAME

_____

DATE

PAWVERBS
~ FOR A ~
CAT LOVER'S HEART

Inspiring Stories of Feistiness, Friendship, and Fun

JENNIFER MARSHALL BLEAKLEY

TYNDALE
MOMENTUM®

A Tyndale nonfiction imprint

Visit Tyndale online at tyndale.com.

Visit Tyndale Momentum online at tyndalemomentum.com.

Tyndale, Tyndale's quill logo, *Tyndale Momentum*, and the Tyndale Momentum logo are registered trademarks of Tyndale House Ministries. Tyndale Momentum is the nonfiction imprint of Tyndale House Publishers, Carol Stream, Illinois.

Pawverbs for a Cat Lover's Heart: Inspiring Stories of Feistiness, Friendship, and Fun

Some of the stories were previously published in *Pawverbs: 100 Inspirations to Delight an Animal Lover's Heart* by Tyndale House Publishers in 2020 under the ISBN 978-1-4964-4105-8. First printing by Tyndale House Publishers in 2020.

Designed by Ron C. Kaufmann

Edited by Bonne Steffen

Published in association with Jessica Kirkland and the literary agency of Kirkland Media Management, LLC.

Unless otherwise indicated, all Scripture quotations are taken from the *Holy Bible*, New Living Translation, copyright © 1996, 2004, 2015 by Tyndale House Foundation. Used by permission of Tyndale House Publishers, Carol Stream, Illinois 60188. All rights reserved.

Scripture quotations marked CEV are taken from the Contemporary English Version, copyright © 1991, 1992, 1995 by American Bible Society. Used by permission.

Scripture quotations marked ESV are from The ESV® Bible (The Holy Bible, English Standard Version®), copyright © 2001 by Crossway, a publishing ministry of Good News Publishers. Used by permission. All rights reserved.

Scripture quotations marked GNT are taken from the Good News Translation in Today's English Version, Second Edition, copyright © 1992 by American Bible Society. Used by permission.

Scripture quotations marked MSG are taken from *The Message*, copyright © 1993, 2002, 2018 by Eugene H. Peterson. Used by permission of NavPress. All rights reserved. Represented by Tyndale House Publishers.

Scripture quotations marked NIV are taken from the Holy Bible, *New International Version,*® *NIV.*® Copyright © 1973, 1978, 1984, 2011 by Biblica, Inc.® Used by permission. All rights reserved worldwide.

For information about special discounts for bulk purchases, please contact Tyndale House Publishers at csresponse@tyndale.com, or call 1-855-277-9400.

ISBN 978-1-4964-6024-0 Hardcover

Printed in China

28 27 26 25 24 23
7   6   5   4   3   2

For Sephy and Bully

(and their humans who love them so much)

INTRODUCTION

WHILE I WAS COLLECTING STORIES for this devotional, a friend commented that this book would surely be harder to write than my previous one *Pawverbs for a Dog Lover's Heart*. When I asked why, she answered, "Well, most dogs seem hardwired to demonstrate positive traits, but cats are, well . . . just, cats."

I chuckled at her analysis. But the truth is, cats being cats not only made this project enjoyable but also brought surprising depth and complexity to many of the stories.

As I wrote, I began to notice that it was the cats' complexities—and their unwillingness to fit into a one-size-fits-all mold—that continually directed my heart to God and encouraged my soul.

You see, I like for things to fit nicely into boxes, categories, and molds. Categorizing things helps me understand them better. Helps me make sense of them. Which, of course, works well for culinary spices, laundry piles, and story ideas. But not so much with cats, or people for that matter. And definitely not with God.

As you might have noticed, God does not fit into a box. He cannot be categorized, condensed, or compartmentalized. His ways are hard to understand. Sometimes they are impossible to understand. He is strong and yet gentle; powerful and yet meek; sovereign and yet gives us free will. He is just and yet delights in lavishing grace upon us. God is more complex than we could ever fully explore.

The more I wrote about cats and their unique attributes, the easier it became to stop trying to force God and his ways to fit into the confines of my limited understanding. After all, if I can accept that a cat is complex, why would I think that the God who created them would be any less so?

It might sound ridiculous to say that writing about cats has helped expand my view of God, but it did—and it continues to do so. And I pray this book does the same for you. Within these pages you will find a collection of stories based on real-life cats, each one highlighting a principle or lesson found in the book of Proverbs.

Several of the stories in this book are based on personal stories of cats I've had throughout the years—including Foxy, my current stray-cat-turned-beloved-pet. Many other vignettes were inspired by friends, family, coworkers, and fellow cat lovers.

Along with the stories and photos, you will find "Paws & Ponder" and "Paws & Pray" sections at the end of every story. These sections were designed to help you go deeper into the story. To help you look past the surface in order to see a spiritual truth that might impact your own heart.

My prayer is that, as you read, you will find encouragement, laughter, inspiration, and some new friends. And that you might start seeing your own pets as potential teachers—with paws. Who knows, maybe you will be so inspired that you will decide to invite a new feline friend into your life—one who will leave precious little paw prints on your heart and enlarge your own view of God.

Much love,

Jen

MR. CATTYPANTS

When you tell the truth, justice is done, but lies lead to injustice.

PROVERBS 12:17, GNT

"WHAT IN THE WORLD is making that sound?" Liz asked her husband, James. "It sounds like a cow impersonating a siren."

Liz pulled the curtains back but couldn't see past the torrential rain that had turned the evening sky ominous.

"I'll go check it out," James said, taking a flashlight from the shelf.

"Can we come?" pleaded their seven-year-old twins, Molly and Michael.

"I come!" two-year-old Emma echoed, refusing to be left out of the adventure.

"You guys stay here. I'll be right back," James instructed.

"What do you think it is?" Molly whispered.

"A dinosaur!" Emma shouted.

"It's not a dinosaur," Michael corrected. "Dinosaurs died a long time ago—like two hundred years ago!"

Before Liz had a chance to set the record straight on the demise of the dinosaurs, James reappeared with a wiggly mass of wet fur in his arms.

"Kitty!" Emma squealed, her chubby fingers reaching for the cat.

James was soon surrounded by six eager hands wanting to pet the trembling cat in his arms. Liz ran to get some towels.

"Let's give the poor thing some room," she said, wrapping a brightly colored beach towel around the orange-and-white cat. His white socks were caked in brown mud.

"Can we keep him?" Molly asked.

"Please, Mom!" Michael chimed in.

"Peeeease, Mama?" Emma's ocean-blue eyes were wide with expectation.

The kids had been asking for a cat for months. Molly had even started praying for one every night. A part of Liz wanted to make their feline dreams come true, but a bigger part of her recognized that the cat in her husband's arms likely belonged to someone else.

"Kids," Liz began, bending down to her children's eye level. "I think this kitty belongs to someone else. He probably got lost in the storm and couldn't find his way home."

Molly's bottom lip began to quiver. As their most sensitive child, Liz suspected Molly's impending tears were as much about her empathy toward the cat being scared and lost as it was to the realization that God had likely not provided a miraculous answer to her prayers for a cat.

"But what if we can't find his owner?" Michael asked. "Then could we keep him?"

Liz glanced at James. He simply shrugged his shoulders and adjusted the bundle in his arms.

"Let's talk about that after we try to find his owners first. Deal?"

James placed the cat on the floor. After several minutes, the cat began exploring. He rubbed his face against Michael's leg, pawed at Molly's shoelace, and ran his tail along Emma's shoulder, which elicited a belly laugh from the toddler.

"He looks like he's wearing pants!" Molly observed, pointing to the large white patch that ran from the middle of his back down both legs.

"We should call him Mr. Cattypants!" Michael suggested.

For the next three days Liz and James posted signs and talked to neighbors about their temporary visitor. Meanwhile, Liz watched her children become more and more attached to Mr. Cattypants.

At the end of the third day, the phone rang. A distraught woman named Amanda said she had found Liz's sign and believed the cat in the photo was her cat, Toby. She explained how he had slipped out the back door when she went to bring in the patio furniture cushions before the storm. She lived several miles away and couldn't believe that Toby had gotten so far.

Liz invited her to come right over.

"There's my sweet Toby!" Amanda exclaimed as soon as she laid eyes on him. She scooped the marmalade-colored cat into her arms.

Emma reached up for Liz to hold her. Michael and Molly huddled close to each other.

Amanda wiped tears from her cheeks, then handed Liz a photo of Toby with her family, which included two children around the twins' age.

"My kids have been heartbroken," Amanda said. She knelt down in front of Michael and Molly. "You are our heroes. Thank you for finding our kitty and for taking such good care of him."

"Emma hero?" Emma asked.

Amanda laughed and touched Emma's cheek. "You are my hero too."

After Amanda left with Toby, Liz snuggled on the sofa with the children and listened as they talked about Mr. Cattypants. Meanwhile, James grabbed his laptop and searched *cats available for adoption* on a cat rescue site.

It looked like Molly's prayers would soon be answered after all.

PAWS & PONDER...

Have you ever faced a situation where you knew telling the truth would result in disappointment or heartache? What did you do? What was the result? How do you find the courage to tell the truth, especially when it's hard?

———————————————————————   ❀   ———————————————————————

Paws & Pray

God, I want to be a person who is truthful and champions justice, even when it may cost me something. And yet I know I cannot do this in my own strength—I need your help. Grant me the courage to always speak the truth in love.

DUSTY'S DEVOTION

The generous will prosper;
those who refresh others will themselves be refreshed.

PROVERBS 11:25

CHERI COULDN'T IMAGINE A CAT being more devoted to a dog than Dusty was to Shatzi. From the moment Dusty joined their household, she had been trying to win Shatzi's attention and affection. Unfortunately for the black cat with the fluffy tail, her efforts often failed to get anything more than a passing glance from the family's loyal and even-tempered Keeshond—whom people often said looked like a cross between a German Shepherd and a Pomeranian.

Eventually, Dusty had taken a new tactic, one that the resolute cat knew would be impossible for Shatzi to ignore. Every morning, Dusty attempted to groom Shatzi while the tolerant dog took her after-breakfast nap.

"I gotta give you points for your tenacity, Dusty," Cheri said as she sat down with her mug of coffee. Dusty was hard at work licking Shatzi's plush, double-layered coat. "That's gonna be quite a hairball though."

Day after day, Dusty would groom her canine sibling, snuggle up to her while she slept, and attempt to bring her gifts from the great outdoors.

One day, after Cheri returned home from a daylong conference, it became obvious that Dusty's devotion had gotten a little out of control. Shatzi was in her crate, and Dusty was sitting in front of the crate, starstruck. Shatzi, however, was cowering and whimpering in the back corner of the enclosure. The reason was evident. Clinging to the metal bars under the crate's roof was a goldfinch—frantically flapping with all its might, so hard that it ruffled Shatzi's fur.

Cheri swallowed the rising panic in her throat. Shatzi was clearly terrified of Dusty's "gift"—and clueless as to what she was supposed to do with it. Meanwhile, Dusty looked as proud as a preschooler awaiting her mother's praise over her latest finger-painting masterpiece.

"Dusty!" Cheri squealed. "Shatzi does *not* want a bird—alive or dead or stuffed! You have to stop bringing her things from outside!"

Dusty leaned over and licked her side. Shatzi let out a pitiful bark that sounded a lot like *out*!

Cheri knew she had to intervene and rescue the bird, so she put on a pair of oven mitts, counted to five, flipped the latch on Shatzi's crate, and reached for the small yellow and black bird, snatching it on her first attempt. She hurried to the back door to set their traumatized houseguest free but came to an abrupt stop. The door was locked and impossible to unlock with her hands in the oven mitts. *Why didn't I think to open it before starting "operation free bird"?* Thankfully, just then her husband, Daniel, walked in from the garage.

"Door!" Cheri yelled.

"What? Why do you have . . ." Daniel started to ask but then quickly put the pieces together. "Dusty?"

"Yep!"

Daniel threw open the back door, and Cheri opened her hands. The bird shook its feathers, looked left, looked right, looked up, and took flight. Cheri then checked on Shatzi, who was being consoled by Daniel—and keeping a wary eye on Dusty.

That evening Cheri typed "how to get a cat to stop bringing unwanted gifts to a dog" into the Google search bar on the computer. But two weeks later, Dusty took care of that herself. After she misjudged a jump and ended up with a cast on her back leg, Dusty was confined to the house. And so, her daily presents for Shatzi ended.

Dusty navigated like a pro while wearing the lime-green cast, but Cheri could tell her little black cat missed being able to come and go through her cat door. On day two of Dusty's convalescence, Cheri watched in amazement as Shatzi dropped her favorite ball at Dusty's feet. The little cat looked adoringly at Shatzi. A moment later, Dusty swatted the ball with her front leg. Shatzi retrieved it and dropped it again. Their slow game of fetch lasted for several minutes before Shatzi lay down next to Dusty.

For the next six weeks, Shatzi rarely left Dusty's side. The two played together, attempted to groom each other, and napped together. Dusty had never been happier.

Or at least she was until the cast came off and Shatzi became the aloof big sister again.

But something had changed. Dusty had experienced a taste of true sisterhood, which—much to Cheri's delight—seemed to have cured her of her gift-giving ways. Now the two siblings seemed content just knowing the other was there.

PAWS & PONDER . . .

In what ways do you think that living generously can lead to a prosperous life? How can you show generosity to someone today? What are some examples of being refreshed by another person? When have someone's actions refreshed you?

--- 🐾 ---

Paws & Pray

Lord, you have lavished me with generous gifts. Thank you for all the ways you provide for me. Often I can get so consumed with my own desires, circumstances, and needs that I forget to extend generosity to others. Please show me how I can be a blessing and a refreshing presence to someone today.

WHERE ARE THE CATS?

Do you like honey? Don't eat too much,
or it will make you sick!

PROVERBS 25:16

JENNIFER SHOOK THE RAIN off her umbrella, then leaned it against the side of her pet-sitting client's house. She retrieved a key from her pocket, unlocked the front door, and entered the dimly lit foyer.

"Plato . . . Aristotle . . . Socrates . . . Jack," she called to the cats she had been taking care of all week.

No response.

"Here kitty, kitties. Where are you?"

Jennifer looked in the kitchen where Plato liked to play with the rug. She peeked in the family room expecting to see Aristotle and Jack wrestling with the curtains. She walked to Socrates's favorite hiding spot behind a potted plant and looked under the dining room table where he would often nap after eating.

No cats anywhere.

She tried not to panic as she mentally retraced her steps from the night before. She had come by at seven and been greeted by four attention-seeking cats. She had cleaned the litter box, scooped kibble into their bowls, put down fresh water, and then played with them for a few minutes. All four had been happy, healthy, and accounted for when she left. *What could have happened?*

She checked the back door. It was securely locked. And all the bedroom doors in the home were closed.

"Kitties?" she yelled, somewhat frantically.

Suddenly, a muffled sound reached her straining ears. But it wasn't a meow or a hiss. *Was that a moan?*

Jennifer willed the sound to repeat again.

There! It was coming from the laundry room.

Jennifer ran to the room and stopped in the doorway. There, lying on the tiled floor, were all four cats—each sprawled with legs fully extended and with the roundest bellies she had ever seen.

"What in the world?" Jennifer spoke softly and knelt down to pet Jack.

The Russian Blue was sleeping in a pile of kibble. Jennifer's gaze followed a path of dry food to the source—an open and empty container lying on its side. Jennifer racked her brain. She thought she had closed the lid securely after feeding the cats last night. Either her memory was going, or the cats had somehow managed to pop off the lid and then feasted nonstop on their plunder.

Jennifer moved to Plato, running her hand over his distended belly. A deep feline moan escaped his half-open mouth, making his long whiskers vibrate.

"Oh, you guys!" Jennifer chastised. "How much did you eat?"

Socrates opened one eye and looked at her.

"Just couldn't stop, huh, buddy?"

The gray cat closed his eye.

"You okay, Aristotle?" she asked, bending down to scratch him between his ears.

The tan-and-white cat raised his head for a moment, before it thudded back to the floor.

After making sure the food-coma patients had fresh water, Jennifer jotted down the name of the food she needed to buy to refill the container. Then she let herself out and drove back home.

When she arrived, she took off her boots and coat and headed straight for the bowl of Christmas candy on the kitchen counter. Instinctively, she grabbed a heaping handful as she walked by. But suddenly a picture of four comatose, gluttonous cats passed through her mind.

She dropped all but a single piece back into the bowl. "Maybe I should just have one today," she said to herself, chuckling.

It's been said that "too much of anything can be bad." Do you agree with this statement? Can you think of an example from your own life when too much of a good thing caused a problem? What do you need to "put back in the bowl" today, in order to maintain balance and moderation?

Paws & Pray

Lord, there are so many good and worthwhile things competing for my time, attention, and resources. Please grant me greater self-control so I know when to say "enough"—even to good things. Help me to choose you first and then trust you to help me balance the rest.

A SPECIAL DELIVERY

Do not withhold good from those who deserve it
when it's in your power to help them.

PROVERBS 3:27

AS SOON AS DAVE SAW the words *Mom and Dad* on his phone screen, he knew something was wrong. His parents never called at this time in the morning. With the country in the middle of a lockdown due to soaring COVID-19 numbers, Dave's mind instantly went to the worst-case scenario.

Will they have to go to the hospital? Do they have enough food in the house? Should I drive to St. Louis to take care of them? Shaking these instantaneous thoughts from his head, he answered the phone.

"Hi, son. Sorry for calling so early, but your mother wanted you to know that Annie passed away last night."

Dave immediately tried to recall a relative or family friend named Annie.

"She died peacefully, but your mom's pretty broken up about it, especially since Annie was our last cat, you know, and the last tangible connection to your grandma."

"Oh, Dad, I'm so sorry."

He had greatly admired his parents for being willing to take in the three cats his grandmother had left to them in her will. While his mom had always been an avid animal lover, his dad wasn't a cat person. But his dad had cared well for the trio of felines, and he had truly grieved alongside Dave's mom when the two oldest cats had died the previous year. Annie had been providing much-needed companionship for the couple, who couldn't get out much to visit friends.

"Will you let Sarah know? I tried to reach her, but I think she must have already left for work."

"I've got it covered, Dad," Dave assured his father before hanging up.

Dave and his wife, Brooke, wished there was something they could do to help ease his parents' pain. But even if they made the five-hour drive to their house, what could they do? *If only we could carry their grief for them,* Dave thought as he dialed his sister's number.

He was surprised when Sarah answered the phone on the first ring since she was a busy veterinarian in Indiana. Sarah inhaled deeply when Dave told her the news.

"Poor Mom and Dad. I think Annie was really helping them cope with everything that's been going on right now. I hate the idea of them not having her."

"I know exactly what you mean," Dave said. His family's animals were providing comfort, distraction, and a much-needed sense of grounding for himself, his wife, and their two daughters. Having someone else to care for—especially someone who wasn't the least bit concerned about viral load count, flattening curves, or politics—helped restore a bit of normalcy to otherwise far-from-normal days. Dave could hear someone talking to Sarah in the background.

"Um, Dave . . . I think a possible solution was just carried through the door. Gotta go. Call you soon."

What in the world did she mean by that? Several hours later when Sarah called him back, he got the answer.

"Sorry about earlier," she said when he answered the phone.

Dave could tell from the road noise that she was driving and using her car's Bluetooth.

"A woman came in with a young orange tabby cat that she needed to surrender. She was so brokenhearted about it. She is a caregiver to several family members who are really sick, and because of the pandemic, money is tight for her, and she just wanted her cat—Peaches—to have a better life with people who could give her the time and attention she needs."

Dave knew where Sarah was going with this.

"I told her I had the perfect couple for Peaches. And after a quick exam, a few shots, and a flea treatment, I'm driving her to St. Louis."

"You know you are amazing, don't you?"

"I do," Sarah said, with a laugh. "But really, it was like God plopped this little one into my day and said, 'Go take her home.' Mom and Dad were so generous to take in Grandma and Grandpa's cats all those years ago, so it feels good to be able to do something for them."

Dave couldn't agree more.

PAWS & PONDER...

Have you received help from someone recently? Did they give of their time, money, or other resources? Did they advocate on your behalf? How did their assistance make you feel? What are some practical ways you could help someone today?

Paws & Pray

Lord, thank you for all the ways you are always there for me. You supply strength, offer peace, and provide everything I need. You truly are my ever-present help in times of trouble. Please open my eyes to see the needs of those around me, and open my heart and hands to be willing to help where I can.

KEEPING WATCH

Joyful are those who listen to me, watching for me daily
at my gates, waiting for me outside my home!

PROVERBS 8:34

PATTY HAS ALWAYS LOVED CATS. To her, a house is not a home unless a cat lives there too. Her home had been feeling especially empty the past year since losing her two senior cats to cancer, their deaths coming just two months apart. So not surprisingly, when her sister called about a ten-week-old male kitten in need of a home, Patty jumped in her yellow Camaro and drove several hours to pick up the Maine Coon mix she named Onyx. Within a few short weeks, Patty and Onyx had formed a strong bond—stronger than she could remember sharing with any other pet.

When the midnight-colored cat was in the house, he was by Patty's side. He followed her, napped with her, draped himself over her as she watched TV, and slept next to her every night. After a few nights of waking up to a small wet spot on the sheets, Patty realized Onyx was a bedtime drooler. But given his sweet temperament, his loyal companionship, and the fact that his nighttime purring soothed her to sleep, Patty was more than willing to forgive him for a little drool on her sheets.

Over time as Onyx grew stronger, more agile, and more comfortable using the cat door Patty installed, he realized he could come and go as he pleased. Soon his curiosity enticed him to venture farther around Patty's property. He enjoyed exploring his surroundings, chasing leaves and insects, hanging out with the neighborhood cats, and occasionally finding a mouse to pursue. But more than anything, Onyx loved trees. He became an avid and adept climber, especially drawn to an old oak at the very edge of the yard. Its branches extended far past the fence line, stretching toward the road.

Patty liked knowing her little feline buddy had plenty to do while she was at work. "I hate leaving you, but someone has to pay for that canned food you like so much," she would say, teasing Onyx before giving him a see-you-soon kiss.

Patty was never quite sure what adventure awaited Onyx each day, but she knew exactly how he spent the end of his afternoons. Because every day as she turned her car onto the road leading to her house, she would see her black cat scamper down the lowest branch of the oak and run at full speed toward the driveway. Rain or shine, sweltering heat or freezing cold, day after day and year after year, Onyx perched himself in the oak tree to await the arrival of his favorite human. And once he reached her, he weaved in and out of her legs, purring and meowing his delight over her homecoming. And each time, Patty would scoop him up, nuzzle his neck, and plant kisses all over his head.

"You are just a fluffy ball of love," she said, wiping away a trail of drool he left on her shirt collar. "Well, a fluffy ball of love and drool."

PAWS & PONDER...

Are you in a season of waiting? Is it a joy or a burden? Consider actively looking for evidences of God's grace in your life and reminders of his presence while you wait.

Paws & Pray

Father, waiting is difficult. It is so easy for me to feel forgotten when the waiting extends past my comfort level. Please remind me that not a moment of my life escapes you; your timing is perfect and is one more example of your care. Teach me to wait for you with joyful expectation. And give me the words to encourage and support others in their season of waiting.

PABU'S ORDEAL

Do not be wise in your own eyes; fear the LORD and shun evil.
This will bring health to your body and nourishment to your bones.

PROVERBS 3:7-8, NIV

KIM SMILED AS SHE WALKED PAST her seven-year-old tri-colored cat, Pabu, and her Labrador retriever mix, Rigby. The two animals had been cordial frenemies since Rigby joined their family as a two-month-old rescue puppy a few years before. Throughout much of the day, Pabu and Rigby ignored each other, but when the mood struck, they would engage in a feline-canine version of tag or, if they were feeling especially frisky, a wrestling match. Their roughhousing always made Kim a little nervous, especially since Pabu was much smaller than his canine brother. But week after week, Pabu would go back for more, sometimes even instigating their play.

"Be nice, you two," Kim ordered as she walked out the back door to do some gardening one July morning.

The first few hours in the summer sun were invigorating, and soon Kim was lost in her tasks of weeding and pruning. It was work that steadied her heart and mind. But once the sun got hotter and the humidity increased, Kim went indoors to cool off.

As she approached the downstairs bathroom, she noticed Pabu lying at a strange angle by the door. His wide-open eyes didn't blink or focus on Kim. And when she picked him up, his body was floppy and limp.

"Eric!" Kim yelled for her husband as she gently cradled Pabu in her arms.

Eric came running, and Kim met him by the back door. He took Pabu from Kim, placed him on the patio table, and pressed his finger to the cat's chest.

"I can feel a faint heartbeat."

Kim wrapped Pabu in a towel while Eric called the emergency vet to let them know they were on their way.

"Please don't die," Kim whispered to Pabu, who was curled up on her lap during the drive. "We love you so much."

On the way, Kim tried to hold on to hope, but when they arrived, that hope began to evaporate after the vet technician rushed Pabu into a procedure room. They hooked him up to various monitors, took blood samples, and examined him thoroughly before wrapping him in warming blankets.

After what felt like a very long time, the vet told Kim and Eric that Pabu was stable. But the cause was still a mystery. "Pabu's symptoms are consistent with toxic poisoning," the vet explained. "Are there any medications or plants in your house that Pabu could have gotten into?" Kim assured her that all their medications were locked up, and because Pabu, an indoor cat, had gotten into every plant and bouquet Kim had ever brought into their home, she no longer kept any plants inside.

"We'll keep administering antitoxins and monitor Pabu overnight. I'll give you an update tomorrow." Unable to say a final goodbye to Pabu, Kim and Eric left with tears in their eyes.

What could he have gotten into? Kim wondered. She worried all night and the next day as they awaited an update.

When the vet called that afternoon, the news wasn't good. Pabu's organs were shutting down.

"There's one other treatment we can try." The vet's calm voice interrupted Kim's panic. "On the off chance Pabu sustained a concussion instead of poisoning, we could administer a medication to reduce brain swelling. Once again, we'll keep him overnight."

A concussion? Kim pondered. *How in the world would he have gotten a . . .*

Just then Rigby walked into the room. Of course. Rigby had never behaved aggressively toward Pabu, but he clearly didn't seem to take his bigger size into account when chasing his feline sibling.

"Yes, please give him the medicine," Kim said.

Neither Kim nor Eric slept well that night, as hope and dread warred within their minds.

Kim's heart raced the next morning when her phone rang and she saw the vet's number pop up.

"It looks as if Pabu's going to be okay!" the technician told her. "When we took him out of the kennel, he walked right up to me and wanted to be petted. You can pick him up in a couple of hours."

"That's wonderful news!" Kim said, waving Eric over.

The couple were grateful for everything the veterinary staff had done. Hours later Pabu was back home, under strict orders from the vet to avoid roughhousing for the near future.

Short of kenneling one or both of her animals, Kim wasn't sure how she was going to accomplish that. And she knew they would never know exactly what had caused Pabu's coma-like state. But it quickly became apparent she didn't need to worry. Pabu's ordeal appeared to have reduced his interest in smackdowns with his brother. Though Pabu's embrace of a more docile lifestyle might have frustrated Rigby just a little, it brought great relief to Kim and Eric.

PAWS & PONDER...

Is there a habit, behavior, or relationship that has been negatively impacting your life? How has it affected you? Have you sought God's wisdom? What steps could you take today toward health and growth?

Paws & Pray

God, I confess I often do things I know aren't good for me and are a poor reflection of you. Please forgive me. Point out where I am weak and give me the strength to change. I want others to know that I have been transformed by you.

GOOD NEWS

Good news from far away
is like cold water to the thirsty.

PROVERBS 25:25

CAT AND HER HUSBAND, AL, knew their cat, Hans, needed a friend. The Ragdoll had come into their lives as a kitten and immediately bonded with their older cat, Katie. But when Katie lost her battle with kidney disease, Hans was devastated. He became clingy and skittish.

At first Al was resistant to the idea of another cat—the pain of losing Katie was still so raw.

But as Hans continued to grieve the loss of his friend, Al and Cat began searching for a younger female on a local Ragdoll cat rescue site.

Unfortunately, only older male cats were available, so they decided to wait and pray for just the right cat for their family.

They didn't have to wait long.

Just a few days after their initial search, they received a message about a three-year-old female blue point Ragdoll named Lily who was in need of a new home. Cat and Al immediately emailed the family to let them know they would love to meet Lily. And then they waited.

And waited.

Cat didn't want to get her hopes up, but at the same time she felt sure that Lily was meant to be theirs.

They prayed again, asking God to bring just the right cat into their lives—at just the right time. Then Cat and Al both went to work and tried not to think about Lily.

When they returned home, there was still no response from Lily's family.

"Perhaps they changed their minds about giving her up for adoption," Cat said.

"Maybe they chose another family," Al said.

Suddenly the phone rang, and Cat answered it. It was Lily's owner. She had been touched by Cat and Al's email and wanted to tell them what was going on.

She explained that when her son returned home from being deployed overseas, his doctor discovered he had a brain tumor.

As the family was processing this news, Hurricane Katrina hit New Orleans and destroyed their home. The family moved to North Carolina to be close to the hospital where their son was scheduled for experimental treatment.

The family had several cats, but Lily was so young that she was having trouble adjusting to all the changes. All she wanted to do was play. But her human family couldn't give her the attention and affection she deserved. They wanted her to go to a home where she could thrive, but they were struggling with the difficult decision to let her go.

Cat listened with humble gratitude for their sacrifice.

"We would like to talk it over as a family this weekend," Lily's owner said, "and then I will call you on Sunday."

And so Cat and Al waited, fearing the answer would be no.

When the phone rang on Sunday, the answer was yes. The family wanted Cat and Al to give Lily a home. Cat tried not to squeal into the phone as they made arrangements for Lily to be brought to their home that evening.

Cat hugged Hans. "You're going to get a little sister tonight," she told him, her voice giddy with excitement.

When Lily stepped out of her cat carrier, she began walking around the house like she belonged there. And from the moment Hans first sniffed her, he would not stop following her around.

Lily's original owners still keep in touch. Cat sends them regular updates about the cat they loved enough to let go. And Cat is delighted every time she gets an update about their son's miraculous recovery. Not only is Lily thriving, but so are two grateful families that have been connected because of her.

PAWS & PONDER...

What good news have you experienced recently? What good news are you longing to hear? In what way is the good news of the gospel like cold water to someone who is thirsty?

_____   ✿   _____

Paws & Pray

Lord Jesus, you provided the best news of all when you defeated sin and death and rose to life. You did all this so that I can have a relationship with God, by believing and trusting in you. Thank you for choosing to lay down your life for me. Father, give me opportunities to share this incredible news with others.

ONE RICH KITTY

Laziness leads to poverty; hard work makes you rich.

PROVERBS 10:4, CEV

TRUDY IS CONVINCED that her Bombay cat, Tuck, has three main goals in life: Stay as close as possible to those he loves—mainly Trudy and his feline sister, Nan; win the affection and adoration of every human he encounters; and chew on every inedible item in the house.

Tuck's affectionate and playful personality more than compensates for any frustration Trudy feels about constantly replacing shower curtain liners, shoe-laces, mini-blind cords, curtains, and more. Plus Tuck seems to have an uncanny ability to sense Trudy's moods and know what she needs from him.

Thankfully, his obsession with tags—on clothing, towels, pillows, and blankets—is limited to the tag itself. However, Tuck's preference for tags emblazoned with the words DO NOT REMOVE has convinced Trudy that not only is her mini-panther able to read, but that he takes those words as a direct challenge.

But after a while, Trudy became weary of Tuck's chewing frenzy, so she banned him from all the bathrooms, bedrooms, and hallway closets. And for those items she couldn't hide or protect behind a closed door, Trudy found an effective solution.

"I wonder if any other house has curtains covered in cat anti-scratch tape," she told Tuck after wrapping a portion of the new panels in wide sheets of double-sided tape.

When she discovered the tape was actually keeping her determined cat from bothering the curtains, Trudy went on a bit of a taping spree, covering the corners of her new coffee table and every visible square inch of her new sofa. The reviews

claimed that the sticky tape should modify a cat's behavior within a year, at which point it could be removed.

Trudy doubts she will ever peel it off. And when visitors come, Trudy throws an old quilt over the sofa to keep their clothes from sticking to the tape.

With the exception of his chewing propensity, Trudy wouldn't change a thing about Tuck. He is the exact cat she needed, even when she didn't know she needed him.

Tuck's desire to be close to her at all times helped Trudy endure the loneliness of the pandemic. His insistence in joining Trudy's video calls for work delighted her team members, especially when Tuck practically lay on the computer keyboard. And his high-volume purr often brings comfort and grounding to Trudy on life's tougher days.

"I really can't imagine not having him in my life," Trudy admitted to a friend who regularly asks about Tuck's latest adventures. "He brings so much laughter and love into my life and to the lives of so many. He really is a one-of-a-kind cat."

One day when Trudy's friends stopped by for a visit, Tuck ran to greet them, then promptly flopped on his back in a not-so-subtle request for a belly rub. One woman was talking to Trudy and not paying attention to Tuck. Trudy held back a chuckle as Tuck scooted closer and closer to her friend, put his paw on her leg, and then flopped onto his back to offer her his belly—all while loudly demanding attention. His antics left the group in stitches.

In that moment Trudy realized that Tuck is a very rich little kitty—rich in adoration and affection. Almost as rich as the little cat has made her and everyone else who experiences his love.

PAWS & PONDER . . .

In what ways do you think Trudy felt rich because of Tuck? What are some ways you feel rich that have nothing to do with money? Did you have to work hard to obtain those "riches"? If so, how? Think of ways you can share kindness, compassion, justice, and love with those around you.

Paws & Pray

Lord, reorient my heart to crave the riches of heaven above the trappings of earth. Let my work make a difference for your Kingdom and benefit those in need. Enable me to work hard, not for selfish gain but as an act of love and worship for you.

BOOTS HAS GOT YOUR BACK

Let love and faithfulness never leave you; bind them around
your neck, write them on the tablet of your heart. Then you will
win favor and a good name in the sight of God and man.

PROVERBS 3:3-4, NIV

MOLLY LEANED against the weathered fence. The sleeves of her thick jacket protected her arms against the rough wood. *If only a jacket could have protected my heart*, she thought as one of her five barn cats rubbed against her leg.

"Hi, Boots," Molly said, bending to pet the gray-and-white short-haired cat.

Boots, barely a year old, still had plenty of kitten energy. After receiving sufficient attention from Molly, he darted off into the tall grass. Molly chuckled as he pounced on a brown leaf and wrestled it to submission.

"Good job there, buddy! Way to get that leaf," she cheered.

It felt good to smile since recent events had been anything but happy. Two weeks earlier, Molly had spoken up against something at work she knew was wrong. But instead of being lauded or listened to, she had been fired—after ten years in a job she had imagined would be her last. Worse than the loss of income, the loss of daily structure, and the loss of friendships was the sense of betrayal she couldn't shake. People she had trusted weren't who she thought they were. And because her job was in Christian ministry, that revelation hurt most of all.

As she stared off into the distance, Molly prayed aloud. "God, I thought I was where you wanted me. What am I supposed to do now? And how will I ever be able to trust anyone again?"

Molly had been repeating these questions for days, but she still had no clear answers. She closed her eyes and rested her head on her forearms. A moment later, she was startled when something fuzzy touched her cheek.

Boots!

"You sure know how to scare a person." Molly looked from the ground to the top fence rail, gauging the distance. "How in the world did you get up here?"

Boots rubbed his head against Molly's shoulder. He cautiously put a front paw on her jacket, then climbed onto her arm, and settled himself into the crook of her elbow. Molly stood perfectly still. The cat provided much-needed comfort.

But after a few minutes, Molly's arm started to go numb from Boots's weight. "Sorry, Boots. Time to get down."

Rather than jump, Boots simply scooted up Molly's arm and settled between her shoulder and neck, purring contentedly.

"Well, instead of a parrot, I have a cat on my shoulder." Molly laughed to herself.

Molly figured that the moment she moved, Boots would bolt, so she slowly stepped away from the fence. Boots didn't move. Molly walked toward her truck. Boots didn't move. She pulled a gardening flat of mums from her truck bed. Boots didn't move.

"Well, I guess we're going to plant these together," she said to the cat, repositioning him around her neck like a feline scarf.

Day after day, week after week, Boots would climb onto Molly's neck as she tended her new garden and prayed about what to do next. He stayed with her as her heart began to heal and as an idea—a dream—began to form. And Boots was there as Molly took the first steps toward a new job opportunity. This new venture was one she never would have pursued without the help of a loyal cat who reminded her daily that God was trustworthy and had not left her.

PAWS & PONDER...

Have you ever felt betrayed? How might meditating on the love and faithfulness of God help you heal from that betrayal? What is one thing you can do today to focus your heart on the love and faithfulness of God?

Paws & Pray

Lord, it is so hard to live on this earth and not experience the sting of betrayal and disappointment. Lift my eyes to see your love and faithfulness, and remind me that you will never betray or disappoint me. Give me discernment to know when to speak up, the courage to do what is right, and the endurance to keep going even when things become difficult.

A SEWER CAT AT HEART

My child, hold on to your wisdom and insight. Never let them get away from you.

PROVERBS 3:21, GNT

JULIE AND TIM UNPACKED the last of their moving boxes, then relaxed on the patio with glasses of iced tea.

"At least we finished that job before school starts on Monday," Julie said, putting the cold glass against her forehead. The hot Texas sun was making quick work of melting the ice cubes.

Neither Tim nor Julie had wanted to move. But the small Texas town they had called home for several years didn't have much in the way of promising opportunities for two young educators. So they had applied for teaching jobs in a larger school district. When the same school hired them both, they packed up their belongings, put a "For Sale" sign in the front yard, celebrated when their house sold quickly, and headed east. It had taken a while, but they were finally starting to feel excited about starting a new adventure with their young sons, Phillip and Madison, and their cat, Prance.

Still the reality of the change started to overwhelm Julie as she sipped her tea.

"Everything feels so different—so odd," she said softly. "Do you think we made the right decision?"

Tim nodded thoughtfully. "I do. It's different, for sure, but we have each other, we have the boys, and we are trying our best to follow God's leading."

Her husband was a man of few words, but when he did speak, his words were usually the very ones Julie needed to hear. Just then, Prance ran to Tim.

"Well, where did you come from, little guy?" he asked, stroking the purring cat. "Feeling better?"

When they had made the decision to relocate, one of the first orders of business was getting Prance neutered. Back at their country house with its sprawling land and lack of neighbors, Tim and Julie hadn't given much thought to Prance's extracurricular activities. But when they realized they would be living in a suburban neighborhood, where Prance's comings and goings could likely result in litters of kittens, they knew the procedure had to be done.

Thankfully, Prance had handled everything well and had plenty of time to recuperate during the long car ride to the family's new home.

But since arriving at their new house five days ago, Julie had noticed that Prance was always nearby, always underfoot. His behavior was unlike the independent, free-roaming cat they had come to know. In fact, two years earlier, when they found the malnourished stray living in a drainage ditch and brought him home, they had come to an understanding: In exchange for food, water, flea control, and affection when he desired it, Prance would keep their home and surrounding property free of rodents and reptiles, while also meeting their boys' request for a pet. While Prance occasionally ventured into the house, he seemed to prefer the great outdoors.

But at the moment, the tiger-striped gray-and-white cat bore little resemblance to the independent stray they had rescued.

Tim gave Prance a thorough petting before heading to the kitchen to help Julie put the dishes away.

Later that evening, Tim and Julie decided to scope out their new neighborhood. The wide streets and large wooded lots provided a beautiful backdrop as they walked and talked about this new chapter in their lives. But Julie sensed they were being followed. She turned around a few times, but there was no one in sight. Finally, almost a mile into their walk, they both heard a rustling sound from the culvert underneath a nearby driveway. Moments later, Julie squealed as Prance jumped from the culvert onto the road.

"Has he been following us the whole time?" she asked Tim.

"It appears so. I guess deep down, he's still a sewer cat at heart," he added with a chuckle.

Prance continued to follow them, via the neighborhood drains and culverts, throughout their walk. And on their next walk. And the next. In fact, every time Tim and Julie left their yard on foot, Prance kept pace underground.

Two weeks after starting their new jobs, Tim and Julie were taking a walk—with Prance following along. They talked about how much they each liked their classes and fellow teachers, rejoiced over how well the boys were adjusting, and started making plans for the holiday season.

After several minutes of silence, Tim smiled. "You know, I think if we stay as close to each other, to the boys, and to God as Prance stays to us, we're going to be just fine here."

Julie nodded and then laughed as she caught sight of Prance creeping his way through the drainage ditch to catch up to them.

"Sounds good to me," she agreed, before adding, "as long as I don't have to crawl through a sewer!"

PAWS & PONDER...

Why is it important to hold on to wisdom and insight? Are you facing something today that requires you to do just that? James 1:5 says that if anyone lacks wisdom, they should ask God, who gives generously. Take a moment and ask God to supply you with the wisdom you need.

Paws & Pray

Lord, you are my Father who knows everything about me. I want to be your student who holds fast to your wisdom and truth. Help me use what you are teaching me to point others to you.

SIMONE THE STAR

Do not exalt yourself in the king's presence, and do not claim a place among his great men; it is better for him to say to you, "Come up here," than for him to humiliate you before his nobles.

PROVERBS 25:6-7, NIV

"I STILL CAN'T BELIEVE you are doing this," Nancy said with a laugh as her sister, Louise, and her friend, Judy, pulled an artificial tree from its box. "It's not even Halloween yet."

Simone, Nancy's Siamese cat, fled from the room as the tree emerged.

"Yes, but you love Christmas, and we love you!" Judy declared, holding the bottom third of the tree as if it were Moses' staff.

Nancy's throat began to constrict from emotion. She rubbed the site of her latest chemo injection, grateful the nausea hadn't hit in full force and yet dismayed she was having to endure the healing poison again.

Thinking about the road ahead made her feel tired. She had mentioned that to Judy several days ago.

"With this new chemo schedule, I'm scared I'm not going to feel good enough to decorate for Christmas this year," she had shared over the phone.

Judy understood her friend's love of all things Christmas. However, Nancy could never have imagined that a few days later her friend would show up on her doorstep like a Christmas sugar plum fairy and declare it decorating day. Louise, who had recently come for a visit, joined right in. And within a few hours, Nancy's house looked like the set of a Hallmark Christmas movie.

Nancy smiled at her friend and her sister, grateful for their kindness..

"Okay, come on, my little elves," Nancy joked. "You need a coffee break."

Leaving the top section of the tree to attach later, the women headed for the kitchen, passing Simone on the way. The playful cat made a beeline for the living room.

"So, how will she do with all the decorations?" Judy asked.

"She's a stinker," Nancy said with a chuckle. "Every Christmas she acts like I put all that stuff up just for her to play with."

The women chatted as they sipped steaming coffee. To Nancy it all felt so normal. So familiar. So . . . healing.

"All right, troops," Judy declared, "that tree is not going to decorate itself. Time to finish the job and stick a star on top!"

As the women walked back into the living room, they came to an abrupt halt, then broke into laughter.

Lying atop the tree—like the Christmas star—was Simone.

"Well," Louise said, "guess you don't need to put the top section on. Clearly, Simone has found the perfect napping spot."

Nancy rolled her eyes. Her kitty's antics never ceased to entertain her.

"Simone, get down!" Nancy commanded, sounding far more amused than stern.

Simone was annoyed at being disturbed. She took her time getting up, stretching and arching her back. Then with a flick of her tail she jumped from her perch and curled up on the tree skirt below.

"From being a star to being a present," Judy said, smiling.

The ladies attached the top section of the tree, filled each branch with ornaments, and secured the star. They then stood back to admire their work.

"It's perfect," Nancy whispered. "I cannot thank you enough."

It was a precious—almost sacred—moment. A moment Nancy would cherish during the difficult days ahead.

Judy looked closer at the tree.

"Is that . . ." she started, pointing at two blue eyes peeking out from the middle of the tree.

"Simone!" Nancy yelled. "Get out of that tree!"

While Simone sought a place of honor in the tree, Nancy was honored by her friend's selfless act of kindness. How can you honor someone today?

Paws & Pray

Lord, I admit that I often want to be the star of the show, rather than following your humble example of servanthood. Jesus, you loved me so much that you left your rightful place in heaven seated next to God and came to earth to die for me. Remind me of that truth whenever I start acting like I deserve to be in the spotlight more than anyone else. I want to be a servant and show kindness to others in your name.

NINJA CAT

Do not plot harm against your neighbor,
who lives trustfully near you.

PROVERBS 3:29, NIV

"DON'T WORRY ABOUT ABBY," Kory's mom said on her way out the door. "I'll feed her and clean the litter box when I get home. She's a good little cat and won't bother you at all."

Kory locked the door behind his mom, then walked down the hall to his bedroom. He had just arrived home after completing his first year of college, and everything—including his mom's new night-shift job—felt different. His siblings had all moved out. His parents had divorced. And his mom now had a cat.

Or at least she claimed to have a cat. Kory hadn't actually seen the cat in the hour he had been home. He saw food and water bowls, a litter box, and a scratching post, but no cat.

It didn't really matter, though. He was starting a new job in the morning at a construction site and needed sleep more than he needed to meet this new member of the family.

Over the course of the next week Kory barely saw his mom—and never once saw her cat. The only evidence to prove he was sharing the house with the two of them was the dirty dishes piled in the sink, tiny pieces of kibble in a bowl, fur stuck to an upholstered chair, and rumpled covers on his mom's bed.

A few days later, Kory was sitting at the desk in his room, working on his computer, when he stopped and looked around. "What is that awful smell?" He rolled his desk chair back, and the odor intensified.

Kory apprehensively peered over the arm of his chair and winced. The source of the offensive odor—something that should have been left in the litter

box—was flattened under the wheel of his chair—effectively and thoroughly smeared onto the wheel and into the carpet.

"What in the world? CAT! Abby, this is disgusting! Where are you?"

Kory jumped up and threw open the bedroom's closet doors. He pushed aside the window curtains. He got down on his hands and knees to look under the bed. He even opened his dresser drawers. But there was no sign of the cat.

As he was trying to decide whether bleach would harm the carpet, he heard a faint scratching sound coming from behind his desk, which was pushed up against the wall. Kory had to crane his neck to see the narrow space behind it.

Standing spread-eagle on hind legs, with her body flattened against the wall and her green eyes focused on Kory, was an orange, black, and white long-haired calico cat.

"Well, you must be the elusive Abby that wasn't supposed to bother me at all. I got the fragrant gift you left me," he scoffed.

Abby held her pose until Kory grew tired of staring her down. He went off in search of carpet cleaner and maybe a respirator. After soaking the carpet with an extra-strength stain remover twice, he used half a can of Lysol to sanitize the wheel of his chair.

The next morning, there was no sign of Abby—or any pungent gifts.

With no further incidents over the next several weeks, Kory, his mom, and Abby fell into a comfortable routine of not seeing much of each other.

One night, after Kory finished a long workday, he dropped onto his bed more exhausted than he had ever been before. His arms ached, and his legs burned. He barely managed to kick off his shoes before crawling under the covers. He was just drifting off to sleep when his feet touched the end of the sheet, which was soaking wet!

Kory jumped from the bed, ripped the covers off, and saw a puddle stain on the sheet that had soaked through to the mattress.

"Abby!" Kory bellowed, storming out of his room in search of the feline perpetrator.

"Who does that!" he yelled into the dark house. "What kind of beast climbs into a man's bed, shimmies under the covers, and decides it's a good place to pee!"

There was no amount of bleach or scrubbing that could get the acrid smell out of Kory's mattress. He was forced to buy a new one that remained safe behind his closed bedroom door.

By the end of the summer, he and Abby had developed a mutual respect for each other. Eventually, she even permitted Kory to pet her with his feet—just far enough away to be within her comfort zone. Kory considered it a détente.

"Well, Abby, I guess Mom was right," Kory told the cat the night before he went back to college. "Other than carpet cleaning, some wet feet, and having to buy a six-hundred-dollar mattress, you weren't a bother at all."

PAWS & PONDER...

In what ways might someone plot harm against their neighbor? Do you think this verse only pertains to next-door neighbors or other people too? What is one practical way you could extend kindness and grace to a neighbor today?

———————————————   🐾   ———————————————

Paws & Pray

Father, you have commanded us to love our neighbors. That includes people in close proximity to me but also strangers I meet. I am often so focused on my to-do lists that I don't take time to slow down and pay attention to others. Allow me to see with your eyes, to love with your heart, and to serve with your hands. And help me to forgive anyone who has wronged me.

WHERE'S JUNEBUG?

Trust in the Lord with all your heart; do not depend on your own understanding.
Seek his will in all you do, and he will show you which path to take.

PROVERBS 3:5-6

MEEOOOW . . .

"Junebug! Where are you?" Dave called out as he, his wife, Brooke, and their daughters searched the house for the orange tabby cat they had rescued several years earlier.

Another muffled meow came from the family room. But there was no sign of the cat. Sawyer and Finn, the two male cats they had kept from Junebug's litter, joined the search by calling out to their mother.

Dave looked under the sofa.

Brooke peered behind the bookcase.

Thirteen-year-old Madelyn took all the blankets out of the large basket that Junebug would occasionally nap in.

And eleven-year-old Ainsley shimmied under the coffee table.

No sign of Junebug.

Meeooow . . .

"The sound seems to be coming from here," Dave said, pointing to an air vent opening in the floor. The family now noticed that the cover to the air vent was lying haphazardly to the side.

Junebug had been playing with the loose cover all week. Dave thought he had secured it the night before, but clearly it had not been fastened well enough for their curious and determined cat. Brooke ran to get a flashlight, but even after shining the light in, they couldn't see Junebug. Sawyer and Finn meowed into the opening. Junebug meowed back.

Afraid that the younger cats would jump in too, Madelyn and Ainsley scooped them up and took them to another room.

Dave and Brooke took turns lowering their arms into the opening, hoping to feel their fluffy cat. They only felt the walls of the air duct. And with no way to access the ductwork from below, there was little they could do but wait for Junebug to find her way out.

"Let's give her a little while to figure things out," Dave suggested. "And if she can't get out, then we'll call someone . . ." he added, uncertainly.

Truth be told, he wasn't sure how the air ducts were connected, what kind of labyrinth Junebug would have to navigate, or if she would even be able to retrace her steps. But while Sawyer and Finn were isolated, Dave quickly pulled all the other vent covers off to give Junebug several different exit options.

Dave could hear meowing and scratching below his feet, but Junebug wasn't visible.

That night Dave slept on the sofa in the family room to be there if Junebug emerged in the quiet of the night.

But there was no sign of Junebug when morning dawned. As Dave drove to work, he contemplated what to do next. Call an HVAC company? A wildlife rescue organization? A spelunker? Why couldn't Junebug have climbed a tree!

When Dave got home that evening, Brooke and the girls reported that Junebug was still trapped and calling for help. Sawyer and Finn—who had been relegated to the second floor—were as agitated as the humans in the house.

"I'll sleep on the sofa again," Dave said, after assuring his family that he would call an animal rescue professional in the morning.

"Okay, Junebug," Dave talked into the hole in the floor. "It's time to come out. You can do it, girl. Just follow my voice and come out." Dave sprinkled a few of the tabby's favorite treats near each vent opening. "Or follow your nose. Just please come out."

Dave waited for several minutes, hoping to hear a meow, a scratch, a hairball being coughed up—anything.

Silence.

Dave eventually lay down on the sofa and fell asleep, murmuring, "Junebug, just follow my voice."

A few hours later he was jolted awake when something pounced on his chest. Junebug!

The prodigal cat dug her claws into Dave's T-shirt and meowed pitifully. A tremble shuddered through her body.

"You're safe, girl," Dave soothed. "You found your way out. But please don't ever do that again!"

While Dave and Brooke wanted to believe Junebug had learned her lesson and would not be diving into any more air ducts, they spent the weekend replacing all the downstairs air vent covers with ones that screwed into place. Dave had learned a lesson from Junebug's adventure too: Never underestimate a determined cat.

PAWS & PONDER...

Can you think of a time in your life when you have felt lost and unsure of which path to take? What did you do? Did you ask God to lead you? If so, how did he guide you in the right direction? And if not, would you consider asking him to do that today?

🐾

Paws & Pray

Father, I am so inclined to lean on my own limited understanding instead of trusting you and asking for help and guidance. Please help me to rely on you more to direct my steps and protect me from making risky decisions.

14

RAFIKI

My child, listen to me and do as I say, and you will have a long, good life.
I will teach you wisdom's ways and lead you in straight paths.

PROVERBS 4:10-11

"OH, BUDDY, I WISH you could understand that I'm doing all of this to help you," Cheri whispered to her cat, Rafiki, as he slept beside her.

Although the beige-and-orange cat seemed to be handling his recent diabetes diagnosis and subsequent treatment well, the regimen was starting to weigh heavily on Cheri. Rafiki didn't fight or scratch or run from her, but she could tell by his wariness that he didn't understand why she was pricking his ears often up to fifteen times a day, wiping his skin with alcohol wipes, or making drastic changes to his diet. He just wanted to play and sleep and sit by her computer while she worked. And Cheri desperately wanted that for him as well.

She loved her little cat's big personality, playfulness, and ability to sleep anywhere. She wanted him to be able to spend his days exploring and finding the most inconvenient and hilarious places to sleep. But it seemed like since his diagnosis, each day was now taken up with his diabetes treatment. The vet had assured Cheri that she wouldn't have to draw his blood as often once they found the right insulin dose and treatment plan for him and that his care would feel much more manageable soon. But those days seemed far, far away. In the meantime, Cheri was still having to prick Rafiki's ear in order to run glucose tests every hour in order to see how his little body was responding to treatment.

Cheri worried that Rafiki would start to be fearful when she approached him. After all, she would definitely become skittish of someone who came at her with a needle every sixty minutes.

But Cheri was committed to doing whatever it took to care for the little

orange cat who had completely captivated her heart—even if it meant causing him temporary discomfort.

Cheri laid her head back on the sofa cushion and watched Rafiki as he slept beside her. His paws twitched a moment before he fully extended his front legs and rested his head against his right leg. Cheri gently rubbed the side of her index finger along Rafiki's leg. He purred in appreciation. In that moment Cheri wished, more than anything, that she could speak cat, or somehow make Rafiki understand.

"None of this is your fault," she whispered. "The diabetes isn't your fault." Cheri cupped her hand and softly stroked his head. "You aren't a bad cat. And I'm not doing this to punish you or hurt you or to be mean. In fact . . ." Cheri gently pulled Rafiki onto her lap, "you are a wonderful cat. So wonderful that I will do whatever it takes to keep you healthy and safe and right here with me."

Rafiki opened one eye and seemed to study her for a minute. Cheri couldn't tell if he was wondering how he ended up in her lap or if he was bracing himself for another poke. But after a moment, he closed his eyes and went back to sleep.

"I know you don't understand, little one, but I do, and you can trust I am doing what is best for you. Always."

As a purr reverberated through Rafiki's body, Cheri leaned her head back and joined her cat in a nap.

PAWS & PONDER . . .

Rafiki had to learn to trust Cheri. Does trusting God come easily to you? Or is it a struggle? What role does trust play in listening to God's instruction? Are you dealing with something today that requires wisdom? Will you take a moment and ask God to guide you?

------------------------------------ 🐾 ------------------------------------

Paws & Pray

Lord, help me believe you always want the best for me—even when my circumstances make it difficult to accept that promise. Incline my heart toward you and teach me to treasure your Word and glean its wisdom. When I grow weary and confused, please make your presence known.

WISE TEDDIE

The wise are cautious and avoid danger; fools
plunge ahead with reckless confidence.

PROVERBS 14:16

IF IT'S TRUE that cats have nine lives, then Teddie was on his eighth. Barb had noticed the young cat wandering in the neighborhood, so she began setting food out for him. That simple act turned into a month of caring for him, including several trips to the vet. More than a month after Barb had distributed countless "lost cat" flyers throughout her neighborhood, she received a call from Teddie's owner, who came and reclaimed his cat.

Two years later, Barb got a call from the vet saying the clinic had her cat. "I don't understand," she said, thoroughly confused. She learned that Teddie had been found more than three miles from her house, again wandering the streets. He had been microchipped when Barb was caring for him, so her phone number was the one on file. Unable to track down the cat's owner, Barb decided to keep the cat, who had acquired several names along the way.

The vet called him Caramel Macchiato. His first owner said his name was Stripes. Barb's sons referred to him by a variety of nicknames, including Tubby. But once he officially became their family's cat, Barb renamed him Teddie.

She had no idea why. He just seemed like a Teddie.

Teddie seemed to adapt fairly quickly to his new home, where he never lacked companionship—neither human nor animal.

Barb and her husband, Brent, were avid animal lovers committed to rescuing creatures in need. Not surprisingly, they had collected a menagerie of pets over the years.

Things were going smoothly . . . but then Brandy became part of their family.

Brandy, a German shepherd/collie mix, was rescued not long after giving birth to a litter. However, her puppies were never found. The loss clearly affected Brandy. She barely ate anything, and she became more lethargic by the day.

Barb's heart went out to the despondent dog.

Weeks later a chihuahua named Woody joined their small pack. Instantly Brandy perked up. She even began to mother the little guy. She cleaned him, scolded him when he got out of line, and tucked him in for the night by wrapping her tail around him. Brandy had clearly adopted Woody as her puppy.

She was the definition of gentleness to the little dog.

But that was not the case with poor Teddie. As gentle as Brandy was with Woody, she was aggressive toward Teddie.

Maybe Brandy had been attacked by a feral cat at some point in her life. Whatever her history was with cats, Brandy decided her current mission was to terrorize Teddie. Between ferocious barking, incessant chasing, and giving him a frightening nip, Brandy made it clear she would not tolerate Teddie being anywhere near her.

Barb tried to play the role of peacemaker and gatekeeper as best she could. Thankfully, she didn't have to assume the role for long.

Teddie quickly figured out how to protect his ninth life by taking up residence in the basement, which was off-limits to Brandy.

From his sanctuary in the basement, Teddie could hear the sound of Brandy's crate being closed and latched. The moment the shepherd mix was secured upstairs, Teddie would quietly venture to the first floor. And if Brandy was spending the night in one of the boys' rooms, the moment the bedroom door was shut, Teddie wandered the halls of the house in peace.

Teddie, the cat with many names and past residences, had figured out how to avoid the dichotomy that was Brandy.

Barb knew Teddie's street smarts—and house smarts—would extend his life and hopefully even give him back one or two.

PAWS & PONDER...

Teddie was certainly not a fool; he realized he would never win over Brandy. Attempting to do so would put him in a potentially dangerous scenario. Can you think of a time when you were uneasy about something and made the right decision to avoid it? What were the results? How might you use caution and discernment in a situation you are facing today?

_____ 🐾 _____

Paws & Pray

Father, thank you for the times you prompt me to carefully think through things and weigh the consequences of my actions. Help me to cultivate this gift by spending time in your Word. If I am headed toward danger, let me hear your voice calling me back to safety.

PUMPKIN

Hatred stirs up strife, but love covers all offenses.

PROVERBS 10:12, ESV

WITH THREE MONTHS TO GO before her high school graduation, eighteen-year-old Hannah couldn't believe what she was hearing. Her school—along with every other one in the district, and most across the country—was closing for in-person learning for the rest of the academic year. The COVID virus that initially didn't impact her world now affected her a great deal. It wasn't just her day-to-day school schedule that was affected, either. She had just learned that two family members were sick, her best friend's grandfather was currently in the hospital, and people she loved were beginning to argue—about social distancing, politics, culture issues, and pretty much everything.

"Mom, what will this mean for graduation?" Hannah asked with concern.

"I don't know, sweetheart."

It seemed every question Hannah asked these days had an "I don't know" answer. Hannah missed the days of certainty and routine.

At first, pivoting to online learning had been fun. Hannah enjoyed sleeping in, attending school in her pajamas, and picking a new virtual background for her Zoom sessions each day. But after a few weeks, Hannah found it was getting harder and harder to stay focused on her schoolwork. Her attention span started slipping, which negatively affected her grades. And she missed hanging out with her friends.

As the school year progressed, everyone started turning their cameras off or angling them upward. Hannah understood. She did it too—it was weird letting all your classmates see your bedroom.

Two months passed, and Hannah faced the fact that she would not get to

attend her prom. And instead of a big graduation ceremony, she would receive her diploma through the car window in a drive-through version of the event. She wondered if she would get a side of fries with her hard-earned certificate.

The big family trip they had been planning to celebrate her milestone was canceled. And while she had been ecstatic to move into her college dorm three months after graduation, now her hopes for a normal college experience were dashed. After only two weeks, the students had to return home, and classes were moved online for the rest of the semester.

Isolation, disappointment, and fear wrapped tightly around Hannah's heart, making it harder and harder to get out of bed each morning.

A few weeks into this strange and lonely reality, Hannah's mom received a text from a friend who had found a flea-infested kitten wandering alone on a street. The friend had rescued the kitten, but she was highly allergic to cats and desperate to find someone to take the orphan.

"All the rescue places and shelters are full," Hannah overheard her mom tell her dad, followed by "So I said we could keep her for a little while—just until a permanent home can be found."

The moment Hannah looked at the little fluff ball, she felt the vice around her heart begin to loosen. Without being asked, Hannah took full responsibility for the kitten—whom she named Pumpkin and easily convinced her parents to let her keep. She fed Pumpkin, cleaned her litter box, played with her, and video chatted with her friends to let them see the adorable little kitten. Day after day as Hannah cared for Pumpkin, she felt the stress and disappointments of the past year begin to fade.

The following year, Hannah was able to return to campus. She was sad to leave Pumpkin but grateful her college was less than an hour away from home.

"I'll be back soon to play with you," Hannah told her fluffy bestie, giving her one last snuggle. As Hannah set Pumpkin down, she looked up and saw her mom fighting back tears. She and her mom had gotten very close over the past year and a half, and Hannah knew her mom was struggling with letting her go.

Hannah hugged her mom for the fifth time in an hour. Then she scooped Pumpkin back up and placed her in her mom's arms.

"Keep her close to you. She's really good at helping you feel better."

Why do you think Hannah responded so positively to Pumpkin? What do you think makes animals so good at helping people through difficult seasons? Can you think of a time your pet helped you through a hard time? How might you reach out in love to someone today?

_____   ❀   _____

Paws & Pray

Lord, you are Love. Thank you for loving your children so much that you offered us salvation and the promise to be with you forever. In a world often consumed with hate, please help me to love as you love and to live as you live so that others might experience your love and find hope.

FELINE FUGITIVES

Whoever walks in integrity walks securely, but whoever takes crooked paths will be found out.

PROVERBS 10:9, NIV

"MARK, HAVE YOU SEEN Frankie or Freddie?" Mia asked her husband.

"Not since early this morning," Mark answered. "Did you check the girls' room?"

"That was my first stop," Mia answered, expecting to find their two tabby cats hiding in the bedroom of their one-and-a-half-year-old twin girls.

The tabby brothers were no strangers to mischief. But now that the human twins could run and climb and feed them table scraps, the feline duo had been inspired to up their mischief game.

After searching the house for Frankie and Freddie to no avail, Mia decided to put LuLu and Laurie down for their naps. *Where could Frankie and Freddie be?* Mia wondered. *They must have found a secret hideout.*

With the girls settled into their cribs, Mia took a cup of coffee and her laptop out to the deck. After spending a few minutes in prayer, she opened the laptop and logged into her email. She deleted four advertisements in a row, then almost spit out her coffee when she read the subject line of the next email from their neighborhood group:

Are these your cats?

Mia had a bad feeling. She chewed her bottom lip as she clicked on the message. A blurry photo of Frankie and Freddie peering into a glass door filled the laptop screen.

"How in the world?" Mia whispered, trying to figure out how her cats had gotten out of the house.

The email explained that Frankie and Freddie had been standing outside said neighbor's glass door meowing loudly and pawing at the door—all of which was apparently sending the neighbor's anxiety-prone cat into hysterics. "Please do a better job of controlling your cats," the irritated neighbor concluded.

Mia wanted to disappear into her chair. How did they get out? How would she get them back? And should she respond to the email? She recognized the neighbor's name. He frequently sent emails about dog owners not picking up after their dogs, people leaving tire marks in his grass, and lawn companies making too much noise in the morning. She decided to wait to respond. But she did need to find her cats—and soon.

Thankfully, she didn't have to worry long about locating the prodigal brothers because the two were back by dinnertime, feigning innocence as they pawed at the back door.

"Oh no, you don't," Mia scolded from the kitchen, as she stirred spaghetti sauce. "You two landed yourselves on the neighborhood's most-wanted list. Don't think you can just stroll back in here like everything's all peachy."

Mia turned the burner down and was wiping her hands on a towel when LuLu toddled into the kitchen.

"Kit-TY," she said, her face lighting up as she pointed to the two felines outside.

"*Mee-ooww*," Laurie called to the duo.

Laurie looked at her mom, then the cats, ran over to the door and pushed down on the handle, opening it enough for Frankie and Freddie to scoot right in.

"Well . . . that solves that mystery," Mia muttered, making a mental note to buy childproof door handle locks.

The handle locks worked well at keeping the cats—and the humans—inside. Mark, however, was late to a meeting because he couldn't figure out how to get out of the house after Mia first installed them. Several months later, Mia decided it was safe to take them off. Surely, Frankie and Freddie's neighborhood mischief had been a one-time thing.

But three weeks later, another neighborhood alert went out about a pair of peeping cats who were taunting indoor cats. Hours later, Frankie and Freddie appeared at the back door of their house without a hint of guilt on their faces.

Mia looked from Frankie and Freddie to their two little blonde accomplices and went to retrieve the childproof locks. This time she vowed they would remain on the door for many years to come.

PAWS & PONDER . . .

What does it mean to walk in integrity? How does walking in integrity enable you to walk securely? What do you think "crooked paths" refers to in this context? What steps can you take today to avoid journeying down a crooked path?

──────────────────────────   ✿   ──────────────────────────

Paws & Pray

God, please walk with me. Keep me far away from paths of temptation, distraction, and sin. I want to be someone with integrity who never lets go of your hand.

18

SEPHY, STOP!

Pay attention to my wisdom, turn your ear to my words of insight.

PROVERBS 5:1, NIV

THERE WERE MANY THINGS Carol worried about when it came to her bobtail cat, Persephone. *Is she eating enough? Is she eating too much? Will she overcome her fear of the window seat? Does she feel self-conscious about her little nub of a tail?* But one thing she didn't worry about was Sephy running away.

Although Sephy was an indoor cat, she enjoyed outdoor adventures. From watching birds and chasing butterflies, to prowling for cicadas and patiently awaiting a view of her chipmunk friend, there was no end to Sephy's natural world entertainment. Occasionally, she liked to venture out to the bushes that bordered their property line or stick her nose through the neighbor's chain-link fence. But most often, Sephy preferred to watch the world from under Carol's chair or while perched on her favorite spot on the deck.

"You're such a good kitty," Carol would often tell her beige-and-gray friend. Sephy was not shy about purring her agreement.

Carol and Persephone had developed quite a bond over the years. Persephone curled up at Carol's feet when she worked, enjoyed walking on a leash with Carol in the park, and patiently sat with Carol as she read. The two seemed to understand each other.

One warm spring afternoon, Carol took her computer outside on the deck and Persephone followed. As she was getting settled, a black cat appeared in their backyard. Startled by the intruder, Sephy let out a deep, throaty meow.

"Now, Seph . . ." Carol started to warn, as she debated her options. *Do I grab her? Do I shoo the intruder away? Do I have time to save the file I'm working on?*

But before Carol could decide on a course of action, Sephy darted from her observation seat and gave chase to the uninvited visitor.

"Persephone!" Carol shouted, kicking off her flip-flops as she joined the game of chase.

As Carol rounded the corner, she spotted Sephy nearing the sidewalk, closer to the road than she had ever been before. Carol's heart plummeted, and her blood pressure spiked. The black cat had crossed the road—and Sephy was about to do the same.

"Sephy, stop!" Carol yelled.

Sephy came to a screeching halt and looked back at Carol. As if realizing where she was, Sephy did a funny little jump and hightailed it back to Carol, who scooped her up in her arms just as a car zoomed by. Carol held her cat tightly to ease her own fear.

"Oh, Sephy, you are such a good girl. Good job listening to Mama!"

Sephy let out a loud meow, which Carol interpreted to mean, "I don't know what got into me, but thank you for stopping me."

"I love you, sweet girl. Now let's go inside because Mama's nerves are shot. But first . . . we have to find my shoes!"

PAWS & PONDER . . .

Do you heed God's voice? Can you recall a time when following his prompting kept you from danger or trouble? What steps can you take today to minimize the noise and distraction of the world and hear what God is saying to you?

Paws & Pray

God, so many things compete for my attention, and so many people's voices urge me to join them. Please help me to keep my ears and heart tuned to you. I want to recognize your voice and faithfully follow you.

19

A LONGING FULFILLED

The hopes of the godly result in happiness, but the
expectations of the wicked come to nothing.

PROVERBS 10:28

"MOM! THERE'S A CAT in our ditch!" twelve-year-old Andrew exclaimed, bursting through the back door. "It's not a fox. It's a cat!"

Ella, eight, jumped up. Her homework went flying as she ran to her brother. "What?" she shrieked. "Are you serious?"

"Come on," Andrew urged. "You too, Mom, come on!"

Jen pushed the cutting board filled with chopped vegetables to the center of the kitchen island—safe from the reach of their counter-surfing Golden retriever, Bailey. She couldn't help but smile at her animated children. They were talking so fast she could barely understand what they were saying. She heard *ditch, bushy-tailed, not fox, cat!*

"We need to get her food," Andrew declared.

"It's a *girl* cat?" Ella shrieked again, clapping her hands.

Andrew nodded. "I think so. It's all fluffy."

Jen thought her daughter was going to swoon.

"A fluffy cat of my very own," Ella whispered.

"Okay, you two," Jen said, trying to temper the escalating euphoria. "The cat probably belongs to someone."

Ella's intense look got Jen's attention. "Mommy," Ella said as if she were talking to a child, "this is the cat we have prayed for. I just know it."

After the children had begged Jen and her husband for a cat for years, Jen finally told her kids that if they ever found a stray cat, they could feed it and

take care of it—outside. Jen had a severe allergy to cats that made keeping a cat in the house impossible.

But that didn't discourage her determined kids. When Andrew was seven, he began praying every night for a cat. Soon his three-year-old sister joined him for the nightly petition. After several months passed without a miracle cat falling from heaven, the siblings' prayers began to dwindle to once every couple of weeks. When several years had passed without a stray cat appearing on their doorstep, their prayers had all but stopped.

But now, taking charge with complete confidence, Ella opened the refrigerator, took out a slice of deli turkey, and announced, "My cat likes turkey."

I guess Ella knows, Jen thought, following her kids outside.

Sure enough, there in the drainage ditch was a cat. The poor thing looked pitifully thin, with leaves and pine needles sticking to her coat and the long fur along her chest. When the three of them approached, she retreated into the large pipe that ran under the driveway. Andrew took the piece of turkey from Ella and squatted in the ditch. He didn't move a muscle.

Within minutes, the nervous cat approached. She took a tentative nibble, then devoured the entire slice. Ella ran in the house to get more. Jen watched as the cat climbed into her son's lap. His face beamed with joy.

Ella returned with the entire package of Boar's Head turkey. Jen started to protest, but she took one look at the poor cat and decided that the least the animal deserved was $10.99-a-pound lunch meat.

Over the next few weeks, Jen sent messages to the neighborhood email group asking if anyone had lost a cat. The family even put up a few signs. But no one ever claimed Foxy, Ella's choice for the stray's name.

A month later, the family was sitting on their back deck finishing dinner when Foxy jumped up on the table. Bailey sprang from her nap to greet the cat with a sniff. Jen still couldn't believe the friendship the two had formed. Ella stroked the cat's thick, soft fur as she silently walked past her plate. Foxy then leapt from the table onto Andrew's lap and began purring.

"See, Mommy," Ella said with a smile. "God sent us a cat. It just took him a while to find us the right one."

Waiting on the Lord is a common theme throughout the Bible. Psalm 27:14 says that a person should "be brave and courageous" as he or she waits on the Lord. Why do you think waiting on God requires bravery and courage? What are you waiting for God to do? Have you grown weary in the waiting? Will you recommit to wait for his leading on a specific request today—trusting his timing and will?

Paws & Pray

God, waiting can be so hard. Would you grant me strength and courage to endure? Help me to trust your timing of the plans you have for me. As I wait patiently on you, help me to encourage others to do the same.

CAN YOU SEE THAT?

A peaceful heart leads to a healthy body; jealousy is like cancer in the bones.

PROVERBS 14:30

MADELINE AND ALEX WERE EXCITED to bring a new kitten home. After rescuing their first cat, Zelda, the previous year, they wanted a second one—both to give Zelda a playmate and because they had joyfully embraced the idea of becoming *cat people*.

They went back to the local shelter where they had gotten Zelda and spent time with many adoptable cats. Madeline wished she could bring them all home, but eventually she and Alex decided on a four- to five-month-old black kitten whom they named Milton. They were excited to bring Milton home and introduce him to Zelda—who welcomed her feline brother with hissing, hiding, and eventually ignoring him.

Milton was perpetual energy covered in black fur. He was the most active kitten Madeleine had ever met, and he brought a heightened and fun level of activity to their home.

Two weeks after they brought Milton home, he was running through the kitchen at full speed and caught his leg on a chair. The moment he got up and started limping, Madeline realized something was wrong.

And it was. Milton had a growth plate fracture in his leg and needed surgery.

"It's a fairly common injury in kittens," the vet told Madeline and Alex. "And a relatively common surgery to fix it."

The young couple loved on Milton one more time before the vet took him back for the procedure, then they went home to await the call that all was well.

Except it wasn't.

During the surgery Milton had a rare reaction to the anesthesia that caused his heart to stop. The team was able to revive him, but Milton's brain had briefly been deprived of oxygen. "I'm sorry to say he likely will be blind," the vet said, explaining the worst-case scenario. "Still, there's a slim chance his eyesight might return at some point."

The couple was devastated. It was bad enough that their energetic little kitten would have to be confined to a crate while his leg healed, but now he would also have to adjust to being blind.

After spending several days in the veterinary hospital, Milton came home. Whenever Madeline looked at him lying in the small dog crate, she felt awful. He had to be miserable in such a small space. *But then again*, she wondered, *what will he do when he gets out? Won't he end up hurting himself again since he can't see where he's going?*

Madeline eventually turned her worries into prayers for Milton's eyesight to be restored. She figured if God said to bring all her cares to him, that included her kitten's eyes. "And God, please give me peace about whatever the future brings."

Eventually, Milton was allowed out of the crate. Madeline didn't know what to expect. Would he be afraid to move? Or would he take off and run right into something? Would he break his leg again?

Milton took a few tentative steps, but within minutes he was navigating the apartment by staying close to the furniture and walls, creating invisible paths. Occasionally, he would bump into something, shake his head or tail, and then simply continue on his way. After several days of exploring each room, Milton seemed to have memorized the layout. Madeline praised his progress. But Milton wasn't done. He didn't want to remain on the floor—he wanted to go higher!

Madeline held her breath as Milton stood in front of the sofa, jumped, and fell back to the floor. "Oh no!" she said, rushing to make sure he hadn't injured himself. The little black cat twitched his tail and tried again. He made it. Day after day, Milton attempted a new jump, fell, shook off his defeats, and tried again.

She had never seen such fortitude. Instead of becoming despondent and immobile, the little fuzzball was resolved to figure out how to live without his eyesight. He even attempted to play with Zelda—who was less than sympathetic to her little brother's situation.

"It's like he's choosing joy," Madeline commented to Alex one night.

A few months after the injury, Milton jumped up on the sofa to join Madeline. Usually he would make his way over and lie down next to her. But this time he climbed onto her lap and began swatting at the red logo on her gray sweatshirt.

"Wait, can you see that?" she asked Milton, quickly grabbing a red bookmark and holding it in front of him.

Milton swatted at that, too.

Later that week, the vet examined Milton and confirmed what Madeline and Alex had prayed to be true. Milton could see!

Madeline couldn't stop hugging her resilient little kitty, nor thanking her prayer-answering Father for caring for the things that mattered to her—especially a little dynamo named Milton.

PAWS & PONDER...

What are some evidences of a peaceful heart? Do you think it's possible to have a peaceful heart in the midst of stressful circumstances? What role do you think prayer plays in pursuing peace? Does your heart long for peace today? If so, will you take a few moments and talk to God about that?

Paws & Pray

Lord, my heart craves peace. Not temporary happiness or a brief respite from stress, but true, abiding, life-giving peace. Peace strong enough to endure all of life's storms. Peace that only you can give. Father, please flood my heart, mind, and body with your peace. I want to inhale your peace and exhale everything else.

GOOD MANNERS BOOTCAMP

A hot-tempered person stirs up conflict,
but the one who is patient calms a quarrel.

PROVERBS 15:18, NIV

WHEN BARBARA'S FRIEND DISCOVERED three emaciated feral kittens living under a rotting shed on his property, Barbara said she would do whatever she could to help them. She had been rescuing and raising cats for more than twenty years, but this would be her first experience with feral cats—cats who are unfamiliar with and wary of humans. While she had committed to help them, she feared the cats, which she named Oliver, Izzie, and Maggie, would be difficult to socialize.

However, ten months had passed, and all three kittens were growing into even-tempered, well-socialized, pleasant cats. And Oliver had quickly become the most affectionate cat Barbara had ever known. The little gray cat sought her out, sat on her lap, slept on her chest, and perched himself on her shoulder. When he was tired or overstimulated, he wanted to be cradled in Barbara's arms and rocked like a baby. Oliver filled up every lonely space in Barbara's heart.

He had also charmed Barbara's thirteen-year-old niece, Katie, who loved helping her aunt care for the cats. Katie, who was often timid by nature, loved carrying Oliver around Barbara's house. She seemed to find comfort and courage holding him.

"Good boy, Oliver!" Barbara would praise him, usually with a giant smile on her face, every time Katie left.

But one day while Katie had Oliver in her arms, he swatted Katie's face without warning or provocation. Startled, Katie dropped Oliver onto the kitchen counter as tears filled her eyes. Barbara noticed a puffy red line near Katie's

bottom lip where Oliver had scratched her. Horrified at her cat's uncharacteristic behavior, Barbara quickly put Oliver in his cat carrier and got some ice and antibiotic ointment for Katie.

Barbara apologized repeatedly to her niece. Katie smiled and attempted to brush off the incident, but Barbara could tell the girl was shaken. Especially when she asked to go home thirty minutes earlier than usual.

That night, Barbara kept replaying the sequence of events before Oliver's attack, trying to determine the reason behind it. She couldn't come up with one. *Maybe it was an isolated incident,* she thought hopefully as she crawled into bed.

That hope crumbled the next day when Oliver, after loudly meowing to be picked up, hit Barbara's face with his paw minutes later. He hadn't meowed or hissed—just struck her cheek, leaving a stingy scratch from his claw. Shocked, Barbara set him down and stood dumbfounded as he scampered off to play with Maggie and Izzie.

Maybe he doesn't like being held anymore.

Later that evening, Oliver cried loudly for Barbara's attention and then purred contentedly in her arms while she watched TV. Grateful that her snuggle-bug was back, she held him close and prayed his brief stint as Dr. Jekyll and Mr. Hyde was over. However, when Maggie and Izzie batted a wadded-up piece of paper into the room, Oliver once again hit Barbara's face.

That was the answer! He swats when he wants to be put down! she suddenly realized, rubbing her cheek.

Now that she was aware of the reason Oliver resorted to bullylike tactics, Barbara formulated a plan to teach him some manners. *Maybe I shouldn't pick him up anymore,* she briefly thought. But Barbara knew Oliver was a cuddle muffin at heart—one who simply needed to learn appropriate behavior in order to keep being his affectionate little self.

Over the next two weeks, Barbara studied Oliver's behavior whenever she held him. She tried to anticipate when he was preparing to swat so she could redirect him or put him down before his paw touched her face. If she didn't catch him in time, she would place him in his cat carrier after he made contact. She also used treats and play time to reward polite behavior. It didn't take long for Oliver to grasp the concept of meowing or wriggling to be put down, instead of swatting.

Two weeks after Oliver graduated from Barbara's good manners training course, Katie returned for a visit. She eagerly greeted each of the cats, but she kept her distance from Oliver. "I'm still scared of Oliver, Aunt Barbara."

"I understand, Katie. Oliver didn't mean to hurt you. But it will take time for you to trust him."

The next week when Katie came to visit, Oliver greeted her loudly, rubbed against her ankle, then sat facing her, clearly wanting to be picked up. Katie smiled and lowered herself beside him. She patted her lap, inviting him to climb up. Oliver happily accepted Katie's compromise and within minutes fell asleep on her lap.

It took several more visits before Katie felt comfortable enough to pick Oliver up again or hold him very long. But Katie hasn't stopped inviting Oliver onto her lap, well outside of face-swatting range.

PAWS & PONDER...

What conflict did Oliver stir up with his face-swatting behavior? How did both Barbara and Katie demonstrate patience? What was the result of their patience? What situation are you facing today that requires patience? What conflict might result if you act rashly?

Paws & Pray

Lord, it is so easy for me to react without thinking, out of hurt and pride. I want my words to be filled with patience, love, and trust in you. Grant me wisdom and discernment to know when and how to speak up and when to remain quiet. And help me be a person who calms quarrels and points others to you.

WATCHFUL REX

The Lord sees everything you do.
Wherever you go, he is watching.

PROVERBS 5:21, GNT

"MOM! REX WON'T STOP STARING AT ME! I'm trying to do my homework, but I can't focus."

"I know the feeling," Shannon mumbled.

Shannon rubbed her neck and took a deep breath. She had been working all afternoon on a document that she needed to complete before a meeting with her boss the next day. But since bringing her thirteen-year-old daughter, Ava, home from school an hour ago, Shannon had been stuck on the same paragraph.

"Ava, Rex stares at everyone," Shannon said, trying not to be irritated by the interruption. "That's what he does. Just try to ignore him. Or go in a different room and close the door."

A dramatic adolescent sigh echoed through the small house, as a muffled middle-aged groan rumbled through Shannon's throat. *Good ol' Rex.*

Shannon loved their six-year-old cat. As a kitten, Rex had been the perfect distraction for her and Ava when she and Ava's dad divorced. The little black cat's playfulness made Ava laugh—which was something she hadn't done much of after her dad walked out the door with no intention of coming back. Shannon still found it hard to laugh since her husband chose his addiction over his family, but Rex's willingness to sit with her in her misery and heartache was a comfort she cherished.

And yet, as grateful as she was for Rex, the cat had an unnerving habit of staring. Maybe it was just that his piercing green eyes made his casual observation of the world around him appear more pronounced. But whatever the reason, his stare was intense. So intense that Shannon was convinced Rex could get a hostile witness to crack with one well-timed stare.

She first noticed his intense stare as a kitten when he wanted to play. Instead of bringing her a toy or pawing at her leg like the other cats Shannon had had over the years, Rex would simply sit and watch her or Ava. He wouldn't meow or move. He would just stare until they stopped what they were doing and played with him.

As Rex matured, his stare grew more extreme.

He would stare at Shannon from the kitchen windowsill while she made dinner.

He would keep an eye on Ava from his scratching post in the dining room while she worked on homework.

He would perch himself on the bookcase in the family room, his penetrating gaze riveted on Shannon and Ava while they watched TV.

And, on more nights than Shannon could count, she would awaken from a deep sleep to two green eyes boring into her unconsciousness.

Rex would even exhibit the same behavior when Shannon's friends came over. One of them was so startled when she noticed what looked like a miniature black panther staring her down that she spilled her drink.

"Rex, buddy, can you turn it down a little?" Shannon would ask—all while Rex maintained unsettling eye contact.

And yet every summer when she and Ava went to visit Shannon's parents, Shannon found that she missed Rex's watchful eyes. It would only take a few days of being without him for Shannon to realize that she longed for her cat and the comfort his unwavering presence brought.

"MOM! He's still staring at me!" Ava's whiney yell broke through Shannon's thoughts.

"Rex, maybe you can dial down the vigilance just a little," Shannon said as she retrieved her watch-cat from his post.

Does knowing God sees everything you do bring you comfort or concern? Why do you think you feel this way? Why is it important to have an understanding of God's character (his love, compassion, justice, sovereignty, forgiveness) when meditating on this verse? Is there a situation in your life that you feel like God doesn't see? If so, how does this verse speak to you in that situation?

Paws & Pray

Lord, this verse from your Word is both comforting and convicting. It's comforting because I can rest in your sovereignty, knowing that you see and understand all things in a way that I simply cannot. And it's convicting because my sin is not hidden from you. Reveal my sin that I might repent and find forgiveness. Wash me clean and comfort me with your presence and love.

SWEET PEA'S MITTEN

The greedy stir up conflict, but those who trust in the Lord will prosper.

PROVERBS 28:25, NIV

CAN THIS WEEK *please go by a little faster?* Carolyn thought as she waited anxiously to bring her new kitten home.

After losing her beloved cat, Winnie, earlier that summer—and grieving more than she had thought possible—Carolyn was ready to bring a new companion into her life. She was delighted when she saw the kitten from the Paws Humane Society online. She just had to wait until the kitten, whom she had named Sweet Pea, turned eight weeks old to bring her home.

In an attempt to keep herself busy while she waited, Carolyn got out needles and yarn and began knitting—something she enjoyed but hadn't done in quite a while. It didn't take her long to create two cute toys in the shape of tiny multicolored mittens, made irresistible with catnip inside. She planned to put one in Sweet Pea's carrier for the ride home and tuck the other in a drawer for safekeeping.

Finally, the week was up. When Carolyn brought Sweet Pea home, the mitten was larger than the kitten's head. Sweet Pea would lie on the mitten like a pillow, cuddle it like a stuffed animal, and curl up on it like it was a tiny bed.

As Sweet Pea grew, she took her mitten everywhere. Wherever she was, her mitten was there too. The mitten became her lovey, her comfort item, and her friend. She would cling to it when she was upset and bring it to Carolyn when Mommy was upset. In fact, it was so cherished that it started showing signs of wear and tear.

Carolyn tried switching it out for the identical match, but Sweet Pea rejected the imposter. After listening to her cat pitifully carry on for more than an hour,

Carolyn made a few repairs to the original mitten and gave it back to Sweet Pea. Her cries became purrs as she nuzzled her treasure.

For three and a half years, as the well-loved mitten began to show its age, Carolyn tried to swap it out with mitten #2, but Sweet Pea would have none of it.

There may be a time in the future when the old mitten will be too far gone. But not now. Her tiny mitten is enough for her.

Sweet Pea trusted Carolyn to take care of her, and she trusted her catnip mitten to comfort her.

Carolyn took this illustration of contentment to heart as she and Sweet Pea moved into their new home two years later. Every time Carolyn started looking for just one more item for the house, she would stop and smile, thinking of Sweet Pea's favorite mitten and questioning the necessity of another household purchase.

Thanks, Sweet Pea, for the reminder. I have everything I need, and it really is enough.

PAWS & PONDER...

What does trusting in the Lord and being content have to do with prospering? In what ways do we prosper by trusting in the Lord and being content? Conversely, how can being greedy or discontent create conflict in our lives?

Paws & Pray

God, I have everything I need in you. And yet I often want more and more material things in order to feel satisfied. Father, fill my heart with an awareness of your presence so that I will focus less on acquiring more things. Remind me of your sufficiency and love and how you provide good things for me. Help me to be grateful for everything you have given me and to be content.

NOT A CAT PERSON

Whoever is patient has great understanding, but one
who is quick-tempered displays folly.

PROVERBS 14:29, NIV

TANA HAD ALWAYS THOUGHT of herself as a strong-willed, non-cat person—until the summer a stray cat showed up at her back door.

The beige-and-black short-haired cat was covered in leaves and wet grass when he appeared on Tana's patio one warm drizzly night. Tana didn't know much about cats, but she recognized that this one was not well cared for. He was thin, and he had a wide scar on his head and a desperate look in his eyes.

"Well . . . hello," she said, startled to find the cat on her patio while taking the trash to the outdoor bin.

The cat made a long, low guttural sound and took several steps back.

"I promise I'm not going to hurt you."

The cat eyed her cautiously as he retreated even farther. Unsure of what to do, Tana placed the bagged trash in the bin and walked back inside, trying to put the mangy little animal out of her mind. But when she went to the sink to wash her hands, she noticed he was back on the patio, watching her.

Moved by his pitiful look and shabby condition, Tana took some grilled chicken strips from the refrigerator and walked outside. She tore the meat into small pieces, laid them on the decorative stone bordering the patio, and went back inside.

Tana watched through the kitchen window. The cat didn't move; he just stared at her.

"Go ahead, eat it," she encouraged him through the glass.

He continued to stare.

Eventually, Tana called it a night. But first thing in the morning, she checked to see what had happened. The chicken pieces were gone and so was the cat.

But later that evening he returned, meowing pitifully. Tana put more cat-sized pieces of chicken in the same place as the day before. This time the cat ate them immediately while Tana watched through the kitchen window. She repeated the routine for two more nights.

On day five, Tana set out a can of cat food. The cat didn't seem to mind the change of entrée or that his server sat on the patio while he ate.

"I think I'm your dinner date, Leo," Tana said with a laugh, using the name she had started calling him.

One night, after finishing a can of salmon, Leo tried to run inside the back door when she opened it.

"Oh no, you don't," Tana said, gently scooting him back with her leg. "I'm happy to feed you, but I live inside and you live outside."

Leo walked back to his little bowl and lay down on the towel Tana had set out for him.

As summer gave way to fall, a cold front brought a series of torrential thunderstorms to the area. Tana moved Leo's bowl under the carport to give him shelter from the rain. She also put a large cardboard box on its side and placed an old comforter in it for bedding.

"There," she said. "Now you have a dry place to sleep."

Leo scarfed down his seafood medley, then walked over to Tana. She ran her fingers through his soft fur and gently scratched his back—which elicited loud purring. But when Leo tried to follow her in the house, Tana put out her hands and stopped him.

"I live inside. You live outside."

Soon winter set in, and as the daily temperatures dropped below freezing, Tana began to worry about Leo. She decided to make a space for him in her laundry room. She set his bowls, a litter box, and his freshly washed comforter in the corner of the small room.

"This is just temporary, Leo," she explained, pulling the pocket door closed. "Just until the weather gets warmer."

Leo purred and rubbed his head on his comforter.

That winter turned out to be one of the coldest on record. One night as the wind howled and the lights flickered, Leo wailed loudly. He sounded terrified.

She brought his comforter into the family room.

"This is just for tonight. Technically, you still live outside."

Several weeks later—with Leo still in the family room—Tana told him good-night and walked into her room. Leo followed.

"Oh no, you don't. This is my room. You stay out there."

And Leo did, for three more nights, until his pitiful cries wore Tana down. With a sigh, she moved his comforter into her room.

"Fine, you can sleep in here, but you have to stay in your bed. The big bed is mine. This comforter is yours. I will not be one of those cat ladies who sleeps with her cat."

The next morning Tana woke up with a soft paw on her face—just like she has every morning since.

PAWS & PONDER...

In what ways did Tana and Leo demonstrate patience? What roles do understanding and self-control play in patience? Likewise, what roles do folly and foolishness play in a quick temper? What situation are you facing today that requires patience? How might you practice understanding and self-control in that situation?

Paws & Pray

Father, thank you for your never-ending patience and understanding. Forgive me for being irritated and quick-tempered with those around me. Help me not to make rash judgments but to see things from other people's viewpoints. Teach me to love and live like you, Lord.

A NEW FRIEND FOR JENNIE

Anxiety weighs down the heart,

but a kind word cheers it up.

PROVERBS 12:25, NIV

"WE'RE MOVING."

Jennie's heart sank the moment the words came out of her best friend's mouth. She wanted to stick her fingers in her ears and hum like she did when she was little, but she was twelve now and knew that ignoring something didn't mean it wouldn't happen. Even if she could block out the heartbreaking words, she couldn't un-see the stack of moving boxes in the corner of Darcy's living room.

The truth was unavoidable. The person she had called her best friend for as long as she could remember—the girl who lived across the street from her, the one whom she had played with, shared secrets with, and pretended was her sister—was moving three states away. And in a world before email, texts, and social media, Darcy might as well have been moving to another country.

Loud meowing interrupted the girls' conversation. Darcy's outdoor cat—one of the many pets her family had rescued over the years—was not so subtly asking for her dinner. Darcy's dad had brought the affectionate gray tabby cat home three years earlier after finding her foraging in the dumpster behind his medical office. She had been nothing more than skin and bones, and Darcy and Jennie had been more than happy to feed her and shower her with affection. Soon the little cat they named DJ was at a healthy weight and making her gratefulness known through a weekly rodent offering at the back door.

Since Jennie's parents were allergic to cats, Darcy and her parents agreed to keep DJ and let Jennie play with him anytime she wanted. Jennie had loved the arrangement. She felt like she finally had a pet! But now it made the thought of Darcy moving that much more painful. Both of her dear companions would soon be gone.

Over the next two weeks, Jennie smiled through her heartache as she helped her friend pack up the room they had spent countless hours in. She feigned excitement for the new adventures Darcy would have—without her. And she tried to savor every moment with DJ.

Jennie fought back tears the night the two families gathered for the last dinner they would share as close friends and neighbors. Jennie didn't want to cry in front of everyone, and yet the burning in her throat was becoming unbearable. How would she survive high school without her best friend? How would she get ready for dances and dates without Darcy's makeup know-how? How would she ever get to rescue another animal again? Jennie was about to flee to the bathroom to cry in private. However, as she prepared to excuse herself from the table, Darcy's dad cleared his throat.

"Jennie, I have an important question to ask you."

Confusion replaced Jennie's rising panic.

"Oh, um, okay," she said, sitting back in her chair.

"I've talked with your mom and dad about this already. But we wanted to see if you would do something for us," he said, nodding to Darcy and her mom.

Jennie couldn't imagine what Darcy's dad was going to say next. She looked quickly at Darcy. *Why is Darcy smiling?* she wondered, quickly turning her attention back to Mr. Smith.

"We don't think DJ will be happy trapped in a cat carrier for two days as we drive to our new house. And we fear she might run away once we get there and try to find her way back here. So we're hoping we could leave DJ with you."

What? What! Is he serious? Were her parents really on board with this?

"As long as DJ remains an outdoor cat, we are good with it," her mom clarified. Both of her parents were smiling.

"Are you sure?" Jennie whispered to Darcy—wanting so badly to have a cat of her own, but not if it made Darcy sad.

Darcy got up and hugged Jennie.

"I am one hundred percent sure! Besides, knowing Dad, I'll have five new cats in a week anyway!" She laughed. "And I want you to keep DJ. It will be like a little part of me gets to stay with you."

Jennie didn't even try to stop her tears now. And she wasn't the only one crying.

Three days later as Jennie waved goodbye to Darcy, the tears fell again. Her best friend was gone. Jennie retreated under the tree she and Darcy had climbed as little kids, trying hard not to feel so alone.

Meow.

DJ! The little tabby cat rubbed her head against Jennie's leg, and jade-green eyes looked up at her. Jennie ran her hand down DJ's back and began relating stories of her adventures with Darcy. "I don't know if I'll ever have as much fun with anyone else." DJ snuggled next to Jennie's leg and purred, and Jennie realized another best friend was lying right beside her.

PAWS & PONDER . . .

What are some encouraging words people have spoken to you? How did their words help? To whom do you turn when your heart is weighed down by anxiety? Can you recall some of God's words that might cheer your heart when you are feeling weighed down? Who could you speak kind words to today?

Paws & Pray

Lord, you know I often become anxious about things I can't change or control. I believe you have the best plan for me. Thank you for the gift of your Word, which reminds me of who you are and how precious I am to you. Help me to recall your promises and give me courage to speak kind words to others who need encouragement.

26

A SOAPY SITUATION

Love prospers when a fault is forgiven,
but dwelling on it separates close friends.

PROVERBS 17:9

JENNIE SURVEYED the supplies she had collected.

Shampoo—check.
Hose—check.
Large galvanized tub—check.
Cat—check.

She looked at her cat DJ—her first real pet—lying in a sunny spot on the brick walkway. Jennie still missed her best friend, Darcy, terribly, but getting to keep the outdoor cat the two of them had rescued together made Darcy's move a little more tolerable. The day after Darcy's family left in their U-Haul, Jennie bought a new set of bowls for DJ. Two days later she bought a little outdoor cushion for the cat to sleep on. And a week after that, Jennie's backyard was scattered with cat toys—none of which DJ ever touched. Much to the dismay of Jennie's mom, DJ seemed to prefer actual rodents to the catnip-stuffed kind. But Jennie loved DJ, and she wanted the full pet-owner experience, which in her mind meant giving her cat a bath.

All of Jennie's friends with dogs talked about giving their pooches baths. *Well, DJ's fur is like a dog's. So she must need a bath too*, Jennie reasoned.

Jennie flipped open the top of the shampoo bottle. She loved the smell of her mom's Prell shampoo. *Maybe if DJ smells like Mom, it will make Mom less allergic to her.* It was a foolproof plan in Jennie's preteen mind.

DJ looked suspiciously at the large tub in the grass.

Should I pick her up and put her in the tub? Jennie wondered, remembering the scratches DJ gave her the last time she tried to pick up the cat. She had learned the hard way that DJ wasn't much of a snuggler.

Jennie opted for good old-fashioned bribery. She poured half a bag of treats into the bottom of the metal tub and waited. It only took a minute for DJ to rise from her half-hearted slumber and launch herself into the tub. As the cat eagerly devoured the treats, Jennie sprayed her with a gentle stream of water. DJ flicked her ears and tail in displeasure, but she continued to concentrate on the tuna-flavored snack feast.

"Aren't baths fun?" Jennie asked, as she squeezed a half-dollar sized amount of Prell on her palm and rubbed her hands together. As soon as she placed her hands on DJ, there was an instantaneous reaction. DJ's head whipped to the left, then to the right. Jennie had just begun to work the shampoo into a rich lather when DJ let out a menacing sound so loud and unnerving that Jennie's hands froze in midair. DJ leapt from the tub and took off in a sudsy blur—leaving a trail of white foam in her wake.

What did I do wrong? Why did DJ growl at me? Where did she go? Will she ever come back?

As Jennie got up to follow the sudsy evidence, her mom rounded the corner.

"What in the world are you—Is that my shampoo?" her mom asked in alarm.

Jennie dissolved into tears as she explained the ordeal.

"I just wanted to take such good care of her that she would never want to leave me," Jennie hiccupped between tears. "But now she's run away and . . . what if she never comes back?"

Jennie's mom hugged her tightly.

"I think you just need to give her some time. Keep putting food out for her, and I'm certain she'll come back."

Jennie wanted to believe her mom, but she hadn't heard the awful sound that had erupted from DJ. Jennie spent the day cleaning out the soggy treats from the tub and hosing the Prell off the brick walkway. The next day, it rained. But when the sun came out in the afternoon Jennie scattered treats around the backyard.

On the third day she sat in the backyard for hours, praying, crying, and missing her cat—and her best friend.

"Darcy would have known a bath wasn't a good idea," Jennie mumbled.

As she pulled at a tall blade of grass, she heard the unmistakable sound of a cat meowing. She peered in the direction of the sound. A moment later a dry and very clean-looking DJ emerged from the bushes.

Jennie sat as still as she could, determined not to spook the cat. Several minutes passed, but DJ eventually began to walk toward Jennie, eyeing her warily. After deducing there was no danger of another bath, DJ—who did smell an awful lot like Jennie's mom—rubbed Jennie's side, then curled up beside her.

"Thanks for coming back," Jennie whispered. "I'm sorry there was so much soap to lick off."

DJ purred contentedly as Jennie stroked her back. And in that moment Jennie experienced the precious gift of forgiveness.

PAWS & PONDER . . .

What does forgiveness mean to you? Why are understanding and discernment key parts of forgiveness? Is there someone you need to extend forgiveness to? Is there someone whose forgiveness you need to seek? What steps might you take toward forgiveness today?

——————————————————— 🐾 ———————————————————

Paws & Pray

God, because you have forgiven me, I know I am called to forgive others. And yet forgiveness isn't always as easy as saying a few words. Please grant me the understanding, discernment, and resolve to offer forgiveness to those who have wronged me—and to seek forgiveness from those I have wronged. I don't want a relationship to end because I failed to take the necessary steps. Show me how to have a forgiving heart toward everyone in my life.

27

A CAT NAMED DOG

We may make our plans, but God has the last word.

PROVERBS 16:1, GNT

"GOD, PLEASE SEND ME A DOG."

At twenty-six, Dana realized she had been praying that same prayer for more than half her life.

From the time she was a little girl, all she could think about was getting a dog. Dogs graced the covers of her notebooks and lunchboxes and were on each of the posters on her bedroom walls. But Dana's younger brother was severely allergic to dog hair, so she knew from a young age that the canine companion her heart longed for would have to wait until she was grown and had a house of her own.

So earlier this year when she moved into a townhouse with a small fenced-in yard, she began praying again in earnest for a dog.

"Please send me a sweet, fun-loving dog who will keep me company and make me laugh," Dana prayed while she scoured dog rescue websites and classified ads.

There was no point in looking at breeders and purebred dogs since her current part-time administrative assistant job paid just enough to cover her bills and put any extra away toward the dental program she was hoping to start in the fall. While her list of possible canine contenders was quite long, by the time she got around to visiting them, the dog was either spoken for or needed a bigger yard or more time than she could offer.

"God, please send me just the right dog," Dana asked one night after learning that a three-year-old chocolate Lab mix she had fallen in love with online had just been adopted.

A few days later as Dana was rushing out the front door for work, she almost tripped over a brown-and-black cat.

"Well, hello," she said, grabbing the railing to regain her balance. "Where in the world did you come from?"

Dana had never seen the cat before, but it looked healthy and cared for, not like a stray. Dana pondered the situation for a moment. *What should I do? If she's lost, I should probably take her inside and put up signs or something. But if she's a stray, she might destroy my house while I'm at work. If I leave her here, she might get even more lost . . .*

Realizing she didn't have a litter box or any clue how to properly care for a cat, Dana wished the cat well and hurried off. But she thought about the little cat all day at work. *Did she find her way home? Is she lost and scared? Did she wander into the road?*

Later that evening, when Dana stopped at the grocery store for a few items, she found herself in the pet aisle, putting an inexpensive litter box, a bag of litter, and some cans of cat food into her cart. *Now, if I ever find another cat in need of help, I'll be prepared*, she reasoned.

And the next morning when she found the cat on her porch again, she was indeed prepared. Dana used the food to lure the brown-and-black-striped cat with a snowy white chin into her guest bathroom where the litter box was already set up.

The female cat was surprisingly loving when Dana petted her. Dana figured the cat couldn't get into too much trouble in the small bathroom while she was at work. As she walked to her car, she saw her elderly neighbor outside watering her plants.

"Hey, Mrs. Dixon, have you ever seen a brown-and-black cat around here?"

Mrs. Dixon frowned. "No, I haven't, but lots of folks will drive out here and dump animals they don't want or can't keep. It's a cryin' shame."

Dana's heart dropped. Did someone just abandon this poor little cat? How could they do that?

While on a break at work, Dana called a nearby vet to ask if she could bring the cat by to check if she was microchipped.

The cat didn't have a microchip, and no one responded to the "cat found" signs Dana had posted around the neighborhood.

Two weeks after caring for the cat, playing with the cat, snuggling with the cat, and deciding to keep the cat, Dana realized her cat needed a name.

"How about DD—for Dana's Dog?" Dana laughed, trying the name out again.

DD purred in agreement. And Dana offered a prayer of thanks to God for her cat named Dog.

PAWS & PONDER . . .

How do you respond when your dreams are dashed? What longing do you have in your heart today that you fear won't happen? Are you willing to surrender that longing—that dream—to God and trust his will and timing? If not, what is holding you back?

Paws & Pray

Lord, sometimes it is hard for me to trust your will, timing, and provision. But I know trust is built when I spend time with someone. Give me a desire to set aside more and more time with you, reading your Word and talking with you. Please draw my heart closer to you so that I may never doubt what you have in store for me.

AN ADVENTURE FOR GUS

A cheerful heart is good medicine,
but a crushed spirit dries up the bones.

PROVERBS 17:22, NIV

"I'M AFRAID IT'S NOT GREAT NEWS," the veterinarian said to Chris and Mary, giving their cat, Gus, a sympathetic ear rub. "The tests confirm a significant heart defect."

After discussing the pros and cons of a complex surgery and experimental medications for Gus, the vet looked apologetically at the recently retired couple. "Why don't you take a few days to think things over, and we can talk next week."

It didn't take Chris and Mary long to reach a decision about the cat who had mysteriously appeared in their barn a month earlier. They would let him enjoy whatever time he had left without putting him through the ordeal of surgery or side effects from strong medications.

Two days after letting the vet know their decision, Chris ran an idea past Mary. "What would you say to giving Gus a grand adventure and making every day count for him?"

"You mean you want to take him with us on the boat?" Mary asked in amused disbelief. "The boat we are going to live on for the next several years?"

"Well . . . why not?" Chris said with a chuckle, excitement brimming in his eyes. "I mean, how many cats can boast they've circumnavigated the world?"

Mary agreed.

The next few months were full of final preparations—the culmination of five years of planning. They sold their house, stocked up on provisions and equipment, said their goodbyes to friends and family, and then finally stepped aboard the *Aquila*, their fifty-two-foot Santa Cruz sailboat—with Gus in tow.

After exploring every inch of the performance cruiser's hull and cabin, Gus pawed at the rigging, sashayed across seats, and then lay regally in the bow.

"I think he approves," Chris said, motoring out of the marina to begin their maritime journey.

The first few days were rough for Gus as he struggled to adjust to life on the water. When the sea got choppy, he refused to eat or use the litter box. He crammed his body into the small, round stainless-steel sink in the aft head whenever the winds picked up. And he left lots of little messes to clean up in the middle of the night. But eventually the cat and the humans settled into a routine.

As the days turned into weeks, and months, and years, Gus experienced moments many humans have never witnessed: fishing from a dinghy in the middle of the Caribbean, watching an annual canoe race in Tahiti, enduring a lengthy required animal quarantine in New Zealand, playing with dolphins off the coast of Tasmania, watching sea turtles swim in Fiji, and surviving a harrowing storm off the coast of Australia.

During the trio's time at sea, Gus became well-known by the sailing community—a small group of fellow circumnavigators who traveled within a few hundred miles of each other. At least once a week, the floating community would anchor their large vessels and congregate in their dinghies, tying them together while they watched the sun sink into the sea. Gus—who often attended the sunset soirees—would jump from dinghy to dinghy, greeting the people and accepting tidbits and treats.

"That is one happy cat," Chris would often hear people remark about their feline companion. It always made him smile. For the fact was, no one knew how long Gus had to live. But the cat embraced each moment as his own great adventure. And in the process, he inspired a small fleet of others to do the same.

PAWS & PONDER . . .

Do you share Gus's view of life that each day is a great adventure? Or does each day feel like a struggle you simply must endure? How would you describe the current state of your heart and spirit? Tell God how you honestly feel and ask him to breathe life and adventure back into your spirit.

Paws & Pray

Lord, my spirit can feel crushed under the weight of daily responsibilities, hurts, and fears. And yet I know this is not how you want me to live. You invite me to give you my burdens and walk in your strength. Please lighten my heart right now. Remind me who you are and who I am to you. I want to experience the grand adventure you have in store for me.

KITTY YODA

Those who listen to instruction will prosper;
those who trust the LORD will be joyful.

PROVERBS 16:20

"NO," ANGIE SAID STERNLY, picking up the plump young cat before she could sink her claws into the sofa. Angie set her down in front of a tall scratching post and gently placed the cat's paw against the rough sisal.

The light-brown cat Angie had affectionately been calling Sandy Claws dug into the sisal post with gusto. "Good kitty," she praised. "See, isn't that so much better for scratching than my sofa?"

"Why do you go to all this trouble?" Angie's friend Sam asked while he pet Kitty Yoda, another one of Angie's foster cats—so named because of his prominent ears.

Angie redirected a third cat, Oreo Mittens, from the curtains and placed him beside Sandy Claws.

"Because I want the cats I care for to end up in their forever homes," Angie answered. "You'd be surprised how many get adopted only to be surrendered weeks or months later because their owners can't deal with their furniture being scratched or their new cat jumping on their table or hissing at their kids."

Angie intercepted Sandy Claws on her way back to the sofa and set her on top of the scratching post. "And while I wish every adoptive family would invest the time to train their new cat, many just don't have the time, knowledge, or patience." Angie wiggled a felt mouse back and forth in front of Oreo Mittens and laughed when he pounced on it. "I just figured if I'm going to foster cats, then I'm going to give them the best chance of staying in their new homes."

Sam scooped Kitty Yoda onto his lap. Angie knew that the affectionate cat had been working his way into her best friend's heart—in spite of Sam's protests that he wasn't a cat person and that his house wasn't cat-proof. The eight-month-old kitten curled up on Sam's lap and purred loudly.

Having picked up on Sam's affinity for the little cat who had been with her the past six weeks, Angie had been working extra hard to get Kitty Yoda ready for adoption—which she hoped would be by Sam. But if not, Angie had no doubt the friendly guy would be adopted soon.

Kitty Yoda had been surrendered by an elderly couple who had taken the kitten in for a friend who couldn't care for him. But when the wife was hospitalized, the husband knew he couldn't properly care for the energetic kitten and stay at his wife's side. Thankfully, he took Kitty Yoda to the rescue organization that Angie had been volunteering with for the past five years.

Kitty Yoda had adjusted quickly to life at Angie's house—and to the two other cats she was fostering at the time. After giving Kitty Yoda several days to acclimate, Angie had begun her kitty bootcamp training with him.

She used positive reinforcement, redirection, and an abundance of patience as she trained her foster kitty to scratch only approved scratching surfaces, to stay off counters and tables, and to tolerate a variety of noises and situations.

Angie would play with the cats and pet them at their scratching posts so that they would connect the structures with a positive experience. When they scratched on the posts, she would reward them with treats. Alternately, whenever they would begin to extend their claws toward the sofa, she would pick them up and move them to a scratching post, where they would earn another treat for scratching there instead.

Angie also worked hard to desensitize her cats to various stimuli like vacuum cleaners, exuberant children, and being put into a carrier. It was often a slow and laborious process, but her kitty bootcamp had proven quite effective. So effective that she had a collection of thank-you cards from happy adoptive families.

"Hey, Ang," Sam said with a tone that made Angie smile. Sam was holding Kitty Yoda up to his face. "You're sure he's not going to destroy my house?"

Angie held up her right hand and swallowed a laugh. "I promise he will not destroy your house."

"This was your plan all along, wasn't it?" Sam asked. "It took you five years, but you finally wore me down. I want Yoda."

And by the way Yoda was rubbing his nose against Sam's cheek, it was clear the feeling was mutual.

PAWS & PONDER...

In what ways did Kitty Yoda, Sam, and Angie all prosper because of their willingness to listen to instruction? Can you think of a time when you prospered because of your willingness to listen to instruction? When have you experienced joy as a result of trusting God? What instructions are you struggling to follow? What small steps of obedience and trust could you take today?

_____   🐾   _____

Paws & Pray

God, please forgive me for the times I have gone my own way and ignored your instructions. I long for the peace and joy that come from obeying you. Continue to teach me. Incline my heart to yours and help me to follow you.

SIMPLE KINDNESS

If you want to be happy, be kind to the poor;

it is a sin to despise anyone.

PROVERBS 14:21, GNT

TINA LOOKED AT THE STACK of bills on the counter. She didn't need to log in to her bank account to know that she wouldn't be able to pay them all this month. Her shoulders slumped as she pulled last night's tuna casserole from the refrigerator. She dished out a serving to reheat in the microwave.

Tina had been working for the past six months as an administrative assistant at a tire store—a big improvement from the late shift she had been working at the pizza place. But money was still tight.

Will I ever get ahead?

When the microwave timer went off, Tina took her plate outside on the deck. Her townhouse backed up to a nature reserve, giving her a glorious view from her backyard.

As she took her first bite, she heard a rustling sound in the bushes. Assuming the noise to be squirrels at play, she continued to eat. But when the rustling turned into a pitiful meow, Tina set her plate aside and stood up to get a better look. A gray-and-white cat emerged from a nandina bush.

"Well, hello," Tina said to the unexpected visitor. "I've never seen you around here before."

She expected the cat to run away, but it didn't even look up. It kept walking toward Tina's deck—its little nose pressed to the ground.

"You're a confident one, aren't you?"

The cat continued walking, lifting its nose every few steps to sniff the air before making it to the stairs of Tina's deck. It cautiously climbed up.

Tina knelt in front of the haggard-looking cat, whose matted fur and notice-able ribs tugged at Tina's heart. She stretched her hand toward the little animal who again raised its nose as if catching a new scent. Now just a foot away, Tina noticed the cat's unfocused, glassy eyes. She snapped her fingers, but the cat did not react at all. Tina surmised the stray could neither see nor hear.

"Oh, kitty," she said. "What happened to you?"

The cat rubbed against Tina's leg, then lifted her nose into the air again—something smelled good.

The tuna casserole.

Without a second thought, Tina put her plate in front of the cat, who devoured it in less than ten minutes. After eating her fill, the cat licked her front paws and then lay down on Tina's outdoor rug.

Tina sat with the cat until the sun dropped below the horizon. Before turn-ing in for the night, she set out a bowl of milk and spread a thick blanket beside the cat.

"Goodnight, little kitty."

The next morning the cat was gone.

Tina hoped she would see the cat again, but she never did. The little cat was a fighter and had clearly found a way to keep going, no matter what life threw at her—a way that clearly included the kindness of strangers.

Three weeks later, Tina opened her mailbox to find a card from an aunt she hadn't seen in ten years. The aunt wrote that she felt led to send Tina a little gift, and she had enclosed a check.

Tina's eyes blurred with tears at this unexpected gift, and she immediately thought of the feline visitor. Maybe Tina's simple act of kindness was being repaid.

PAWS & PONDER . . .

In what ways does being kind to the poor make us happy? Do you think this proverb applies only to those who are poor financially? Who else might need our kindness? What are some practical ways you can show kindness to the poor in your life?

Paws & Pray

God, thank you for caring about me and meeting my needs, often by stirring the hearts of others to help. Please stir my heart to show kindness to the poor—the poor in spirit as well as those struggling financially. Fill my heart to overflowing with love for you so that I can gladly share your loving-kindness with those in need.

FLIGHTY FRIENDSHIP

One who has unreliable friends soon comes to ruin, but
there is a friend who sticks closer than a brother.

PROVERBS 18:24, NIV

BROOKLYN'S FOUR BARN CATS had no idea they weren't chickens. And really, she couldn't blame them. Brooklyn had discovered the newborn feral kittens the same week she received a fresh brood of baby chicks. The two groups had grown up together. In fact, for the first several months of their lives, the kittens and chicks had played together, slept together, and eaten their meals together. Finn, Skye, Panda, and Archie considered the chickens their siblings.

The kittens had also befriended the horses and dogs at the farm, but their favorite playmates were the chickens, whose size, proximity, and lack of teeth made them ideal companions.

But as the chickens grew—or more specifically, as one particular chicken began to grow a rather pronounced red comb on his head and began practicing an eye-opening cock-a-doodle-doo—the dynamics between the furred and feathered siblings began to change.

Jeremy the rooster came as quite a surprise to Brooklyn, who thought she was raising a brood of all hens. However, his affectionate personality, protective nature with the hens, and precision as an alarm clock made him a welcome addition to the farm.

That was, to everyone but the cats.

As Jeremy grew more comfortable in his role as protector of the hens, he grew less tolerant of feline shenanigans. And over time the hens did as well. Unfortunately, their aloofness and annoyance only seemed to encourage the cats to try harder to win back their affection. It seemed that at least once a day Brooklyn was breaking up a dispute between the chickens and the cats.

"Finn, stop chasing Frida!"

"Jeremy, we do not peck our friends—even if they're being annoying!"

"Skye, you are not a chicken! Get out of the coop!"

"This is not what I signed up for when I decided to live on a farm," Brooklyn would often mumble to herself while working through her chores.

One day while she was in the horse pasture scooping manure, Jeremy—flanked by Florence, Frida, and Zazu—chased Finn, Skye, Archie, and Panda into the pasture. The four felines looked up at Brooklyn as if expecting her to discipline their feathered pursuers.

"I'm staying out of this," Brooklyn said with a laugh, dumping the contents of her shovel into the wheelbarrow.

Jeremy and his ladies gave a final flap of their wings and rejoined the others, who were pecking in the grass beside the barn. The cats stood in the middle of the pasture, trying to decide their next move.

As they silently debated their options, two of Brooklyn's mares, Juno and Dakota, sauntered over to investigate the newcomers. Brooklyn smiled wide as the large horses lowered their heads to sniff their feline visitors. Dakota even allowed Panda to rub against her leg.

"Good job, Dakota," Brooklyn praised, walking over to scratch her back. A minute later, she scooped Panda up and let her investigate Dakota's head. "It looks like these two are willing to be your friends. Maybe you should start hanging out here more often."

And they did—when unrelenting rain forced the chickens into their coop for an extended stay. The cats amused themselves by playing in the horses' muddy field, cuffing stalks of hay, climbing up the fence to see the horses, and darting around their legs as the equines drank from the water trough.

The horses really seem to like the cats' company, Brooklyn observed on the third day of constant rain.

But when the weather cleared and the chickens were freed from their enclosure, the cats couldn't help themselves. They ran right into the middle of the foraging chickens and tried to get them to play. Jeremy, clearly not amused, gave a loud warning and then charged. Wide-eyed, Finn, Skye, Panda, and Archie skedaddled to the pasture—straight to the nine-hundred-pound friends who gladly welcomed them.

PAWS & PONDER...

In what ways can unreliable friends lead to trouble? What makes someone a reliable or trustworthy friend? Who do you consider to be trustworthy friends in your life? What is something you can do today to be a trustworthy friend to someone else?

_____ 🐾 _____

Paws & Pray

God, thank you for the gift of friendship and for the good friends you have given me. Help me to always be thoughtful and reliable, someone who puts others first. And above all, help me to seize opportunities to tell others about you—the greatest Friend of all.

RULE FOLLOWER MEETS
RULE BREAKER

*Doing wrong is fun for a fool, but living wisely
brings pleasure to the sensible.*

PROVERBS 10:23

MAGGIE'S FAMILY OFTEN SAID that she was the world's most
well-behaved dog. At the mature age of six, the highly sensitive black Lab had
learned each family member's routine, knew what they expected from her, and
was always eager to please.

She was also very good at reading people's emotions and body language—so
good, in fact, that it could sometimes be a problem. For example, if someone in
the family got upset about something, Maggie assumed they were upset with her.
She would be overcome with imagined guilt and run away, curl into a ball, and
make herself as small as possible.

It often took a while to convince Maggie to come out of her self-imposed
time-out. But once she did, she quickly went back to her sweet-natured, obedi-
ent, docile self.

Maggie's highly ordered and rule-following world was working just fine.

And then Gypsy the kitten blew into Maggie's well-ordered life like a tiny
tornado, tossing mischief around like flying debris.

The first week, Gypsy explored the house and found many interesting things
to play with . . . like the dial on the gas fireplace! With a flick of her paw, the
fireplace turned on, melting the decorative candles inside into puddles of wax.

The black-and-gray-striped prankster upped her game by figuring out how to take stoppers out of bathroom sinks and ricochet small items—oftentimes earrings—down the drain.

She continually hid small items like hair ties and earbuds in secret nooks and crannies throughout the house.

Gypsy's mischievous ways frustrated her human family, but no one was more bothered by her antics than Maggie—who grew increasingly anxious about Gypsy's blatant disregard for rules and order.

Maggie would pace when Gypsy was on the prowl for kitten-sized trouble. She would whine when Gypsy seemed to find the trouble she was looking for. And the Lab would run and hide the moment her humans discovered a Gypsy-sized mess.

Her owners would continually reassure her that they knew who the true culprit was. "Oh, Maggie girl, we know you didn't do it."

Maggie would lick and nuzzle her humans as if trying to apologize for Gypsy's behavior.

And Gypsy? She did not seem the least bit concerned by her family's frustration. Instead, she would sashay right by Maggie, undoubtedly in search of another bauble to plink down a drain.

PAWS & PONDER...

Did you see yourself as Maggie or Gypsy in this story? Have you ever done something foolish and actually enjoyed it—at least for a moment? In what ways can living wisely bring pleasure? Do you think that living wisely means never having any fun?

---　✿　---

Paws & Pray

Lord, I want to be wise, but far too often I'm not. Sometimes, in the moment, my foolish choices seem fun, but the feeling doesn't last. True lasting joy is found in you. Help me to be mindful of that truth and be sensible when I have a decision to make.

A HOST OF GOOD NEIGHBORS

*A good name is more desirable than great riches; to
be esteemed is better than silver or gold.*

PROVERBS 22:1, NIV

LINDSEY'S PHONE CHIMED with a text message from her next-door
neighbor:

Our yard is being sprayed today.

She sent a thumbs-up emoji.

"Well, Bea, no front yard time for you today. But that's fine. We have lots to
do inside anyway."

Lindsey's cat meowed softly, then pawed at her favorite toy. While Beatrice
played, Lindsey went back to work.

An hour later Lindsey's phone chimed with a text message from another
neighbor.

Spotted a hawk while walking Max.

Thanks! Lindsey texted back.

"I wonder if any other kitties have their own neighborhood watch patrol," she
called out to Beatrice, who was sprawled out in the middle of the floor, sleeping
with her head on her toy.

It touched Lindsey's heart deeply to know how much her neighbors cared
about her little cat. With very few fences in the neighborhood, Lindsey often
found herself chatting with neighbors while she worked in her garden, when she
went to get the mail, and when she sat outside with Beatrice, who loved watching
birds, observing squirrels, and befriending bunnies. A gentle soul by nature, Bea
never tried to harm any of the visitors to her backyard. She hadn't even tried to
chase the mouse that made its way into their house a few months earlier.

Lindsey loved her cat's tender nature, and so did the neighbors who met her. "Your cat is so sweet," the neighbor across the street commented.

"I just love when Bea comes over to say hello to me," her next-door neighbor often said, beaming.

"I wish I had a cat like Bea," a young neighbor a few houses away frequently sighed.

When pandemic restrictions kept Lindsey and most of her neighbors at home for several months, Beatrice's popularity rose even higher. Her visits became the highlight of her neighbors' days. And many of them began looking out for Bea—texting Lindsey when their lawns were being treated with chemicals so Bea wouldn't get sick; alerting Lindsey to hawks, coyote sightings, and loose dogs; and sending her news articles about cat food recalls.

At one time, Lindsey would have described Beatrice as shy and timid around other people, but not any longer. She blossomed during the pandemic—soaking in the attention and affection of her neighbors, bravely interacting with the dogs next door, and politely demanding that Lindsey include her in business Zoom meetings so she could say hello to Lindsey's coworkers.

Each day brought a new adventure, and every time Lindsey would watch her companion make a new friend or coax a smile from a weary face, she would thank God for her little cat—who had no opinions on the latest controversy storming through social media, but who simply offered her friendly presence to others. And whose name her neighbors had learned.

"It's been a really hard year for most of us," Lindsey told Beatrice while fixing her dinner one night, "but you have made it a little bit better for a bunch of people. Good job, Bea."

PAWS & PONDER...

In what ways is a good name better than riches? How does someone earn a good name? Who do you think of when you read Proverbs 22:1? Why did you think of them? What do you hope people think about you when they hear your name?

Paws & Pray

God, your name is holy, above all other names. Your name is worthy of worship and praise. Help me to remember your name as I interact with those around me. Teach me to pursue integrity, faithfulness, and humility as I strive to be an ambassador who shares you with others.

FINDING FORREST

If you become wise, you will be the one to benefit.
If you scorn wisdom, you will be the one to suffer.

PROVERBS 9:12

IT WAS GETTING CLOSE to Christmas, and the Hutchins family hadn't seen their cat, Forrest, in days. Ever since they had found the tan, gray, and black tabby two years ago living in the woods behind their house, he had shown up on the back deck for dinner every day. Forrest was an affectionate cat who let his adopted family love him back.

At first, the family didn't worry too much about Forrest's absence. They figured their tough cat could take care of himself. But as one day turned into two and two into three without any sign of him, they began to worry.

On Christmas night, they heard a louder-than-normal yowl coming from the back deck. When twenty-year-old Matt opened the back door, he found Forrest standing there, shaking and wide-eyed. Then Matt noticed Forrest's fur was matted with blood from a wound on the cat's neck.

"Quick!" Matt yelled to his family. "Forrest is hurt!"

Matt carefully picked up the cat. His mom, Barb, was already in the garage making a bed for Forrest out of a discarded box that had contained a beanbag chair. She put a flannel sheet and an old comforter inside. Matt gingerly laid Forrest inside.

"Oh, he smells awful," Barb said, sighing. "What on earth happened to him?"

Samantha, her sixteen-year-old daughter, came into the garage with some pieces of turkey from their Christmas dinner and a bowl of water. She hand-fed Forrest, who gulped everything down. "He probably hasn't eaten for days."

Barb called the emergency vet and got instructions for keeping Forrest as comfortable as possible. After a family discussion, they agreed it would be less stressful to keep Forrest at home and have a mobile vet come to them.

"Yes, Forrest was definitely attacked by another animal," the vet concluded, after cleaning the wound. "It could have been a fox or a dog, or possibly a raccoon."

Thankfully, Forrest was current on his rabies shots, so the vet gave Forrest a shot of antibiotics.

"Call me if there are any problems," the vet said.

For the next week, Forrest stayed in the garage, feasting on leftover turkey, using a litter box, and lapping up lots of extra attention. Eventually, the wound healed, and Forrest was ready to return to the outdoors.

At first, he seemed thrilled to be back outside as he ran straight to the edge of the woods.

Matt watched Forrest stalk a robin in the underbrush and silently rejoiced when the bird flew away before Forrest got too close.

Before long, Forrest was on the deck, napping in his favorite spot.

But as the sun disappeared below the horizon, Forrest began yowling and scratching at the back door. The moment Barb opened the door, Forrest ran inside and straight to the door leading into the garage.

"A little scared to be out there tonight, huh, bud? You'll be safe here," she said, opening the door. Forrest ran straight to his king-size bed and snuggled in for the night.

The Hutchins family never found out what happened to their cat during those few days before Christmas, but it seems Forrest has not forgotten. He now sleeps in the family's garage every night.

"You think Forrest knows that whatever hurt him is still out there?" Samantha asked Matt.

Matt smiled. "Well, it's that or he discovered the comfort of a soft bed and regular tasty meals. Either way, he's a pretty smart cat."

Have you ever suffered because you acted foolishly? Can you think of a specific benefit you received when you acted more wisely? Why is it often hard to change our behavior, even when we know we should?

—————————————————— 🐾 ——————————————————

Paws & Pray

Father, never stop teaching me. Please help me to fill my mind with knowledge and to use that knowledge when it's needed. When I wander into danger, please draw me back to you. Help me to be an example to others.

"I'M JUST HERE FOR THE CATS"

Every word of God proves true.
He is a shield to all who come to him for protection.

PROVERBS 30:5

"WHOSE HOUSE IS THIS AGAIN?" thirteen-year-old Ella asked as she stood with her family outside of a two-story white French Colonial in Key West, Florida.

"Ernest Hemingway's," her eighteen-year-old brother, Andrew, answered. "He lived here with his wife Pauline from 1931 to 1939."

Ella spun around, surprise lighting her eyes. "How did you . . .?" And then she spied the informational sign her brother was reading from. "Cheater!" she teased.

Jen laughed at the playful banter between her two children.

"And Ernest Hemingway was a famous author, right?" Ella clarified.

"Yep. You'll read *The Old Man and the Sea* in school next year," Andrew replied.

"I've never heard of his books before," she said with a shrug. "But it doesn't matter. I'm just here for the cats."

It was the third day of their seven-day family getaway in the Florida Keys—a trip to celebrate Andrew's high school graduation. And while Jen knew that neither of her kids were big fans of touring old houses while on vacation, she suspected the six-toed cats that occupied Hemingway's house would intrigue them. Jen watched her son point something out to his sister.

How did it go so fast? Jen wondered for the hundredth time. *I was just dropping him off at kindergarten. How could it be time for him to go to college?*

A familiar tightness gripped Jen's throat as a barrage of what-ifs began their assault.

What if he's not ready?

What if we didn't teach him everything he needs to know?
What if he turns his back on what we did teach him?
What if . . .

"Uh, Mom?" Andrew asked, interrupting her thoughts.

He nodded to the person awaiting payment for their admission tickets to the house.

"Oh, sorry," Jen said, handing her credit card to the petite woman.

Stepping through the front door of Ernest Hemingway's Key West home was like stepping back in time. Jen could easily picture the author pacing the wood floors as he contemplated his latest manuscript, throwing open the front door to welcome friends for dinner, or relaxing on the front porch.

"Mom! I found a cat!" Ella squealed.

Jen found Ella crouching beside a beige-and-black striped cat. The cat had the strangest paws Jen had ever seen. They appeared to have a fur-covered thumb. Ella's face was beaming.

After spending several minutes photographing and petting the unique-looking and docile cat, they continued their self-guided tour. Each room seemed to contain more cats than the one before. Three cats slept soundly on Hemingway's bed. Four dozed in the cordoned-off kitchen. Two were stretched out precariously along the windowsill in an upstairs washroom. And two more kept watch from under the claw-foot tub.

"So, how exactly did they all get here?" Ella asked, as she paused to pet a black-and-white cat lying underneath a movie poster for *A Farewell to Arms*.

Andrew had read every informational sign in the house and scanned their QR codes, so he had the answer on his phone:

"Hemingway got his first polydactyl cat—that's what the six-toed cats are called—from a ship captain. Hemingway liked the cat so much that he asked the captain to bring him another one when he returned. And then another. Pretty soon the writer had lots of them. Oh, by the way, they don't all have six toes, but they all carry the gene for it."

Jen read a nearby sign out loud. "Hemingway had a hard life and fought a lot of demons, but he found comfort in his cats. He promised that he would always take care of them and provide a home for them."

"Looks like he kept his promise," Ella said.

When the family ventured outside, there were cats everywhere they looked. Some slept under trees, others along walkways, and a few were curled up in front of headstones in the cat cemetery.

"You really did keep your word to them," Jen whispered reverently, running her hand over a heart etched into a headstone.

As Ella and Andrew went off in search of more cats, Jen knelt down beside an orange tabby cat. As she stroked the cat's thick fur, she smiled at the image of her eighteen-year-old son running excitedly with his little sister through Hemingway's gardens.

"God," she whispered in her heart, "I know you love him even more than I do, that you have a plan and a purpose for him, and that you keep your promises. Help me to take you at your word. And help me to trust you to hold him close so that I can start to let go."

Jen wiped her eyes before joining her kids.

"Want to head over to the gift shop to get one of Hemingway's books?" she asked, throwing her arms over her kids' shoulders.

"Nope," Ella said without hesitating. "I'm just here for the cats."

PAWS & PONDER . . .

Spend time reflecting on some of God's promises in the Bible. If you need inspiration, consider Isaiah 41:10, Jeremiah 29:11, Psalm 32:8, Matthew 11:28-29, John 3:16, and 1 John 1:9. Which promise speaks most clearly to your heart today? Do you trust God to keep his word? In what areas do you need help to trust him more?

Paws & Pray

God, every word you speak is true. Every promise you make is good. Lord, I give you my doubts, my fears, and my insecurities, and I ask for your peace, joy, and strength in return. Whisper your promises to my heart and help me cling to them.

LEO'S TACO TRUCK

The name of the LORD is a strong tower;
the righteous man runs into it and is safe.

PROVERBS 18:10, ESV

WHEN KATHY'S COWORKER, SHARON, presented her with a corrugated cardboard cat nook and scratching post in the shape of a food truck, she had to keep from rolling her eyes. It wasn't that she didn't appreciate the gift—she did. And it wasn't that she didn't love her cat, Leo—she did. It was just that the bright blue, orange, and yellow van-shaped box didn't exactly blend in with her decor. However, since she and Sharon were both avid fans of tacos and food trucks, Kathy began setting up Leo's taco truck as soon as she got home. She felt quite proud of herself when she managed to assemble the two-foot-long, eighteen-inch-tall El Gato Fish Taco food truck in less than an hour.

"What in the world is that monstrosity?" her husband, Matt, asked when he came home later that evening.

"Oh come on, it's kind of . . . cute . . . ish. In a tacky, obnoxious kind of way," Kathy replied, unable to hold back her own laughter. "Sharon gave it to me—well, to Leo—and I figured I should at least let the cat see it and decide if he likes it."

However, Leo, who was scared of new furniture—as well as groceries, loud noises, ringing cell phones, and his own shadow—was nowhere to be found.

"Well, I guess Leo isn't really feeling the food truck vibe today," Kathy said with a sigh.

That night as Kathy got ready for bed, she tried hard not to think about the week ahead—specifically the doctor's appointment she had been dreading the past six months. Although her last results had been clear, her body still bore evidence of the cancer that had taken three surgeries and months of radiation to get under control. And while everything was beginning to heal, her mind still struggled with deep wounds and nagging fears. Every pain, every cough, every ache seemed like an assault by an enemy lying in wait, biding his time until he could turn her world upside down again. Kathy's appointment at the end of the week, which would confirm or deny the presence of cancer cells, felt like both a blessing and a curse. Living in the unknown was torture—but what if knowing was worse? She couldn't go through that again. Could she?

The next day, as Kathy and Matt were getting ready for work, she was surprised to find Leo perched atop his new food truck.

"Wow! Look at you, all brave on your taco truck." Kathy stopped to stroke Leo's head, then left the cat to explore it more. "Have fun. I'll see you later, Leo."

Kathy had just gotten into her office building when the sky grew dark. Several minutes later her phoned buzzed with a severe thunderstorm warning. It stormed all day long.

Poor Leo, Kathy thought, knowing how anxious her cat became during storms. *Why didn't I check the weather before I left?*

Leo tended to channel his anxiety into destructive behaviors such as shredding curtains, chewing on mini-blinds, or leaving evidence of his stress on the carpet, so Kathy normally put him in a bathroom if the forecast called for storms.

Kathy took a deep breath before entering the house that evening, trying to prepare herself for whatever she would find inside.

There was no sign of Leo. Nor any sign of feline stress. No shredded or chewed-up window treatments, no laundry strewn about, and no messes on the carpet.

"Leo?" Kathy called. "Where are you?"

Kathy started to fear the worst. *Can a cat have a heart attack from anxiety?*

But before her thoughts could spiral too far down that path, she heard a faint muffled meow. Kathy looked behind the sofa, under the chair, and finally . . . in the taco truck.

There, pressed against the back corner, was Leo.

It took a minute to coax him out, but when she did, Kathy held him and told him what a brave cat he was.

The next day, when Kathy opened the door for the dishwasher repairman, Leo took one look at him and ran straight to his taco truck.

"Looks like you've found your safe place," Kathy observed a few minutes later, kneeling beside the truck to pet her cat through the window opening. Her phone chimed with a reminder of her doctor's appointment the next day. Kathy inhaled deeply and prayed for peace, as well as a good report. She leaned her head into the taco truck. "Got any room in there for me?"

PAWS & PONDER...

When life gets hard, where do you run to? Who or what is your safe place during a storm? How is the name of the Lord a strong tower? In what ways does the name of the Lord keep us safe? Have you found refuge in the person of Jesus? If so, how has that changed your life?

———————————————————   🐾   ———————————————————

Paws & Pray

Lord, there is no refuge that can compare to you. Jesus, you are the strong tower my soul needs. Help me run to you for peace, comfort, healing, and help. I draw courage from you. And even when I can't see through the storm clouds, help me to know that you are with me and that I am safe.

TINY TIM'S TINY TOWEL

*Better to have little, with fear for the LORD, than to
have great treasure and inner turmoil.*

PROVERBS 15:16

PAM STARED AT THE TINY, malnourished black cat that the veterinarian had placed in her arms.

"At first, I didn't think he was going to make it," Dr. Stephens said. "But he's a fighter."

Pam had never intended on rehabilitating and fostering cats. But several years ago, after discovering an injured gray-and-black cat in her backyard, nursing her back to health, and then finding the cat a loving home, it seemed as if every stray cat within a ten-mile radius knew about the lady in the beige ranch house on Birch Street who had a soft spot for unloved cats. And if the cats didn't find her themselves, Pam's veterinarian friend of the past ten years was eager to pass along their request for help.

The little black cat squirmed in Pam's arms. She could feel every one of his ribs. As Pam's heart ached for the neglected cat, her mind went to the three butterballs she was currently fostering. Each one had come to her malnourished and weak, but all had quickly gained weight and confidence under her care. She was hopeful they would soon find good homes, but until then they would have to adjust to Tiny Tim—as Pam decided to call this little guy in her arms. He didn't have a limp like the beloved character from one of her favorite novels, *A Christmas Carol*, but the name just seemed to fit.

As Pam left Dr. Stephens's office with her new charge, her phone dinged.

Max and Sydney's offer was accepted, the text from her mom read. **We're having a celebratory dinner tomorrow night at 7.**

Pam wanted to be happy for her brother and sister-in-law's new house, but it was hard to muster the feelings. Their current house was twice the size of hers. She couldn't imagine what this new one looked like. Pam buckled the carrier into the back of her sedan and headed home.

She loved her brother and was glad he had a job he liked that paid him more money in one year than she would make in five as a middle school science teacher. But when was it ever going to be her turn for a celebratory dinner? Or a new house? Or a car with less than 100,000 miles?

Tiny Tim let out a pitiful mew as Pam turned into the driveway of her nine-hundred-square-foot house.

"Welcome home, little one," Pam said. "It's not much, but it's ours."

Einstein, Newton, and Ms. Curie, the three cats Pam had been fostering the past five weeks, met her at the door. The trio of orange-and-beige cats sniffed the carrier as Pam walked Tiny Tim to the laundry room, a quiet place for him to adjust to his new surroundings away from the other three cats.

As the tiny cat crept from the carrier, Pam gasped at how scrawny he was in comparison to the other cats. Pam set out Tiny Tim's food and water and gave the litter box a shake before sliding the pocket door closed. She put her ear to the door and could hear a faint crunching sound. *Eat up, sweet Tim.*

Einstein, Newton, and Ms. Curie demanded their bowls be filled too.

"Okay, okay," Pam said, surrendering to their persistent yowls.

As the trio made quick work of their dinner, Pam eased the pocket door open to check on Tiny Tim. The little black cat was curled up on a dishtowel Pam had tossed in the room earlier. She had aimed for the washing machine but missed. "I won't disturb you, little guy," she whispered, smiling to herself as she slid the door shut.

The next morning, Pam found Tiny Tim lying on the same towel—even though she had put a new cat bed in the laundry room for him. Einstein, Newton, and Ms. Curie loved their beds, but Tiny Tim seemed content on the small gray stained towel. *You're welcome to it.*

Days later, even after being greeted by Einstein, Newton, and Ms. Curie and checking out their beds, Tiny Tim still preferred his dish towel to his cat bed. He also seemed to prefer his little towel to the toys Pam offered him. The other three cats wrestled, chased, and pawed at the toys, but Tiny Tim was content to watch from his small piece of cloth.

A month after bringing Tiny Tim home, Pam stood in the foyer of her brother's massive new house, feeling pangs of jealousy and insecurity. But then she pictured Tiny Tim's little towel and smiled. *Thank you for showing me what contentment looks like, Tiny Tim. I'm grateful for my little house with lots of room for cats.*

PAWS & PONDER...

What do you think the phrase "with fear for the LORD" means in Proverbs 15:16? How might having a correct view and reverence for God and his sovereignty affect our contentment? How might having an incorrect view of God and his sovereignty lead to inner turmoil?

Paws & Pray

God, please forgive me for running after things that don't honor you. Help me to see you as you are—the almighty, holy, righteous God who loves me more than I will ever be able to comprehend. I want to know deep in my soul that even when I may have little in the world's eyes, I am rich beyond imagining. You are my greatest treasure.

"WHAT HAPPENED TO YOUR CAT?"

The words of the reckless pierce like swords,
but the tongue of the wise brings healing.

PROVERBS 12:18, NIV

NOELLE BASKED IN THE WARMTH of the afternoon sun at the park. It seemed everyone was enjoying the weather. The normally quiet park was abuzz with activity as fellow sun-seekers jogged, walked, and pushed strollers along the tree-lined pathways.

"Doesn't the sun feel good, Penny?" Noelle said, winding her cat's leash around her hand.

She enjoyed these leisurely excursions with her tiny companion, allowing Penny time to attack a clump of grass or roll around on the sidewalk. The fresh air was invigorating.

As Noelle watched Penny explore, she heard someone say, "What a little cutie pie you are!"

A woman approached and knelt next to Penny. She began purring and rubbing against the woman's leg. Then she flopped down and rolled onto her back for a tummy rub.

"You're so sweet," the woman said, laughing.

Penny was just getting started with her repertoire of tricks. She rolled back over and got up to demonstrate her ninja-like moves, culminating with a pounce on a stick. Noelle smiled and thought, *I never get tired of seeing this.*

But when she heard a gasp from the woman, Noelle mentally prepared herself for the words she knew would come next.

"Oh my goodness, what happened to your cat's tail?" the woman asked, standing up and backing away.

I really need to get a T-shirt printed with the explanation, so I don't have to keep saying this, Noelle silently lamented.

"Actually, nothing happened. She's a bobtail—a breed known for their short, stubby little tails. Her tail just happens to be extra short—a little nub," she said, wiggling the tip of her thumb in the air.

The woman kept staring at Penny's back end. "The poor little thing! How awful." The pity in her voice was unmistakable.

Ouch.

Noelle's grip tightened on Penny's leash as the little ninja sauntered to the sidewalk.

After completing a perfect roll, Penny turned toward the woman and waited to receive another belly rub. Instead, the woman gave Penny a quick pat on the head, wished Noelle a good day, and left.

Penny looked at Noelle, her expression saying, "Why didn't she pet me longer? Did I do something bad?" Noelle was used to this reaction from strangers, but it broke her heart to see her cat's confusion. One minute, people were showering Penny with attention, and the next, they were suddenly hurrying away.

Oh honey, people can be so oblivious to how hurtful their words and actions are. I would be devastated if someone rejected me for being different.

"Just because she's different doesn't mean there's anything wrong with her," Noelle almost shouted out loud.

She picked up Penny and whispered in her ear, "You are the cutest, most talented, and most wonderful cat in the world. I love you." Noelle kissed the tip of Penny's nose. "Personally, I think tails are highly overrated. Don't ever stop being you."

PAWS & PONDER...

Has your heart ever been pierced by reckless words? Or been healed by compassionate words? Why do words wield so much power? What words are you longing to hear today?

Paws & Pray

Father God, speak your words over me today. I want your truth to be louder than any other words I hear. Lord, please heal the wounds I've been carrying from other people's words. And may I use your words to bless others.

LOOKING FOR MISCHIEF

There is surely a future hope for you,
and your hope will not be cut off.

PROVERBS 23:18, NIV

"CAN WE KEEP HIM, DAD? Please!" eight-year-old Amy begged, unable to take her eyes off the orange-and-black cat that had followed her father home from work.

"We can keep *her*—while we try to find *her* owner," her dad clarified.

Amy jumped up and down. "But what if she doesn't have a family? Then can we keep her?"

"Try not to get too attached to the cat, Amy," he said. But it was too late. Amy had already envisioned herself playing with the cat, whose half-black, half-orange nose delighted her and made her want to copy the cat's look on her own face with finger paints.

Amy half-heartedly helped her parents hang signs around the neighborhood—and then had to resist ripping each one back down. But when several weeks passed without anyone contacting them, Amy became more confident that the little bicolored cat was theirs to keep.

Because of the cat's knack for getting into trouble, Amy's family began calling her Mischief. She certainly lived up to her name. She dug up plants, sharpened her claws on the outdoor furniture, left hairball confetti on the deck, and dropped various offerings at the back door.

One day Amy's dad came home with a flea collar for Mischief.

"If we're going to keep her, it's our responsibility to take proper care of her. And that means helping her get rid of those pesky fleas," he said, slipping the white collar around her neck.

Mischief wasn't happy with the collar. She meowed loudly while attempting to scratch it off. Amy tried to reassure her kitty that the collar was for her own good, but Mischief still tried to get it off.

Eventually Mischief adjusted to the collar, and they all settled into a nice routine. But one day, several months after the family officially welcomed Mischief, the orange-and-black cat disappeared. They couldn't find her anywhere. The signs they had once posted to find her owners were now hung up in the hopes of finding their cat.

But Mischief was gone.

Amy was heartbroken. She missed her cat and feared something bad had happened to her. And while life went on and Amy found comfort in her friends and being busy with school, her young heart ached for little Mischief.

Two months later, Amy glanced out the back door. "Dad!" she squealed. "Come quick! I think . . . Mischief is back!"

Amy ran outside after spotting a familiar orange-and-black shape walking in their backyard. The cat was a little thinner and missing her flea collar, but otherwise she looked fine. Amy picked her up and squeezed her tight.

"Oh, Mischief, don't ever leave us again!" she said.

Over the next few days, Mischief fell right back into her routine. She would play with Amy after school, take her meals on the back deck, and try—often successfully—to sneak into the house to sleep at night. She even tolerated the new flea collar Amy's dad put on her. Amy felt like all was right in her world once again.

But several months after finding her way back home, Mischief disappeared again. Amy hoped her cat would return like last time—which she did. And like the previous time, she returned without her flea collar.

Disappearing and reappearing became Mischief's pattern. Amy's family never could figure out where their cat disappeared to for months at a time, or how she managed to get her collar off. But in the end, it didn't matter. They were just happy to have her back home—and would always open their arms and hearts wide to receive her.

PAWS & PONDER...

In spite of disappearing for long stretches of time, Mischief was always welcomed back—her hope of returning home was never cut off. Have you ever felt like your hope was cut off? What is the future hope to which Proverbs 23:18 is referring? How can the promise of a future hope help you endure a difficult season?

_____   🐾   _____

Paws & Pray

Lord, with so much brokenness, heartache, sickness, and grief in this world, it can be hard to feel hopeful. And yet my hope is not in this world. My hope is in you. Would you lift my gaze above my circumstances, my doubts, and my fears and allow me to see a glimpse of you today? Remind my heart that my hope—my home—is in you.

BUTTER KITTY

Many will say they are loyal friends,
but who can find one who is truly reliable?

PROVERBS 20:6

ELEVEN-YEAR-OLD AIMEE was excited to move into a new house—although technically it was not a *new* house. It was an old farmhouse. But with its weathered white paint, cheerful blue shutters, and cozy fireplace, it looked a lot like something from one of Aimee's storybooks. Aimee hoped, with all her heart, that this move would be the beginning of a happily-ever-after for her family.

"Do you think Mom and Dad will fight as much, now that we're in a bigger house?" Aimee asked her older sister a few nights after moving in.

Her sister simply shrugged and said, "Probably."

The next morning while Aimee was playing outside, she saw a sign across the street for free kittens. Aimee ran back into the house.

"Can I please have a kitten?" she pleaded. "I'll do everything to care for it."

Her parents agreed, but on the condition that the cat stay mainly outside. Aimee ran across the street to look at the kittens. They were several months old, and Aimee giggled as they tumbled over each other. She eventually decided on a female orange tabby cat and named her Butterscotch. Aimee made a cat bed from old towels and set it beside two bowls on the back porch. Butterscotch quickly took to her new home, but her favorite place was always in Aimee's lap.

Over time, Butterscotch—or Butter Kitty, as Aimee soon started calling her—started venturing farther and farther into the yard with Aimee. Butter Kitty hunted for mice and chased anything that fluttered by while Aimee enjoyed the quiet of the woods—far away from her parents' arguments.

"Butter Kitty!" Aimee would call as she closed the door on the latest confrontation taking place inside the house.

Without fail, the little orange cat would come running right to Aimee whenever she called.

"It seems like all they do is fight," Aimee whispered to Butter Kitty one day as the pair lounged under her favorite tree.

Butterscotch nuzzled closer, then eventually crawled onto her lap. Aimee loved feeling the steady, rhythmic movement of Butter Kitty's breaths. Oftentimes, when she was upset, Aimee would try to breathe in and out exactly like Butter Kitty.

But when her parents announced they were separating again, Aimee cried so hard that even Butter Kitty's soothing breaths couldn't calm her down. She cried until she had no tears left. Butter Kitty never moved from Aimee's lap. Through the flood of emotions. Through the mess of her friend's runny nose. And even through the temptation of a taunting squirrel.

Aimee thought her heart would break when her mom delivered the news that she and her sister would be moving out of the farmhouse and into an apartment with her. That meant Aimee would only get to see Butter Kitty on alternating weekends and holidays.

"Who will care for her and love her? What if she leaves?" Aimee expressed her worries to her sister, who tried to reassure her that everything would be okay. Still, her words did little to allay Aimee's fears.

But Butter Kitty never left. In fact, every time Aimee returned to the farmhouse and called for the orange tabby, the cat would come running—many times springing from a nearby bush or hedge as if she had been awaiting Aimee's return.

With each visit—no matter how much time had passed—Aimee and her feline friend would pick up right where they left off.

"I love you, Butter Kitty," Aimee would often proclaim while the two played together outside.

And she did. She loved her cat so much that when Butter Kitty got hit by a speeding car and had to have her jaw wired shut to heal, Aimee spent several weeks out of her summer caring for her. Since Butter Kitty couldn't eat normally, Aimee would dip her finger in high-protein canned food so the cat could lick it off. Butterscotch made a full recovery.

Years later Aimee went off to college. But every time she returned to the farmhouse for a visit, Butter Kitty would come running when she called.

"I think you're happier to see that cat than you are to see me," her dad would tease.

And while Aimee would disagree with him, deep in her heart she knew that there was a bit of truth to his statement. Butter Kitty had been her constant companion and safe place for more than half her life. It was a love so strong that when Aimee got married after college, Butter Kitty came to live with her and her husband in their new home.

After all, Butter Kitty had always been home to Aimee.

PAWS & PONDER...

Who came to mind when you read Proverbs 20:6? What makes a loyal and reliable friend? Why are those types of friends so important? How can you be a loyal and reliable friend to someone today?

———————————————— ❀ ————————————————

Paws & Pray

God, thank you for the faithful friends you have placed in my life. Help me to be a loyal and reliable friend who keeps confidences and asks for forgiveness when I fail. And Lord, thank you for being the one Friend who will never leave me or forsake me, no matter what I've done.

SMALL PROTECTOR

The wicked flee when no one pursues,
but the righteous are bold as a lion.

PROVERBS 28:1, ESV

AS A YOUNG CAT, Tater Tot wasn't what anyone would call bold or asser-tive. The little multi-colored cat preferred quiet solitude to boisterous gatherings and a familiar blanket to a brand-new toy. In fact, Lynn often wished her petite cat would be a little braver and more animated, especially when she brought home something she thought her pet would like. Invariably, Tater Tot would sprint away from anything new as if the item posed a threat. Such was the case with the window seat Lynn had installed. She had high hopes that Tater Tot would enjoy watching the birds from a higher and softer surface than the floor. However, instead of springing up to the cushion, Tater Tot was terrified and ran straight to Lynn's bedroom, burying herself under the blankets on the bed.

"Oh, Tater Tot," Lynn sighed in defeat.

But several months later, Lynn began noticing subtle changes in her normally apprehensive cat.

It started when Tater Tot showed interest in a long feathered stick toy Lynn's coworker had given her. When Lynn held it just out of Tater Tot's reach, the cat had walked toward it, instead of immediately retreating.

"Wow! Brave girl," Lynn had praised.

A few weeks later, Tater Tot eagerly approached a visitor to their home whom she normally hid from. *This is wonderful progress*, Lynn thought.

And several weeks after that, Tater Tot unexpectedly jumped on the window seat she had avoided for nearly a year. Lynn watched quietly, pretending to act indifferently to her cat's sudden act of courage, but inside she was shouting for joy.

More time passed. One evening when Lynn got home from running errands and pulled into the driveway, she noticed the outside lights on both sides of the garage door weren't working. Normally, they automatically went on when it started to get dark. Lynn knew who to call. Her stepdad knew how to fix just about anything.

"It might be the timer. I can come by tomorrow around three," he kindly offered.

"Unfortunately, I have conference calls all afternoon," she said, fearing the repair would have to wait.

Her stepdad chuckled. "Well, unless you have electrical skills I don't know about, I think I can manage just fine on my own. Just leave the garage door open for me."

The next day, Lynn sat down for a long afternoon of phone meetings. Twenty minutes into her second call, Tater Tot—who had been sleeping soundly beside Lynn's feet—jumped up on the desk and startled Lynn. The little cat let out a deep sustained meow that sounded threatening.

"Are you . . . growling?" Lynn asked aloud, forgetting she was on the phone. "Uh, sorry," she said to her colleagues. "I need to step away from the meeting for a minute."

Tater Tot crept toward the side door leading into the garage and repeated the menacing sound. It was unnerving to Lynn, especially coming from her normally timid cat. Tater Tot crouched low to the ground as if preparing to launch herself at anyone who dared to cross the threshold. Her panther-like pose alarmed Lynn. *What if there was a burglar in her garage? Wait*, Lynn interrupted her own emotional tailspin and looked at her watch. Three o'clock.

"Okay, Killer, you stay here a minute," Lynn instructed Tater Tot, who let out another throaty growl. "Goodness, you are kind of terrifying for a nine-pound cat."

Lynn opened the door a few inches and peeked out. Her stepdad waved.

"Go back to your calls," he said. "I've got this."

Tater Tot tried to dart around Lynn's legs and into the garage to confront the intruder.

"Wow, you conquer one window seat and suddenly you have the courage of a tiger! Down, girl. We're safe."

Tater Tot kept watch by the door for several minutes before she joined Lynn in the living room.

Lynn didn't know what had caused her small companion to go from scaredy-cat to fearless protector. But knowing Tater Tot had her back brought a smile to Lynn's face—and a large helping of treats to the guard cat's belly.

PAWS & PONDER...

Can you think of a time when you had to act boldly? Does boldness come easy for you, or do you struggle to be brave? What role does righteousness play in knowing when and how to act boldly?

_____   🐾   _____

Paws & Pray

Lord, please help me know when and how I should act boldly. Show me when to speak up and how to take action when necessary. Give me your discernment to detect danger and give me the courage I need to speak your truth to others.

SKY'S ROOM

The glory of the young is their strength;
the gray hair of experience is the splendor of the old.

PROVERBS 20:29

"SKY DOESN'T LOOK GOOD TODAY," Phil commented to his wife, Lisa, before leaving for work.

Lisa's heart sank. The truth was, their fourteen-year-old Ragdoll cat hadn't been looking well or acting like herself for several weeks. The once affectionate, playful feline, who had always been underfoot and looking for an available lap, recently had been hiding, hissing, and barely eating. A battery of tests at the vet's hadn't revealed anything out of the ordinary for a geriatric cat. But Lisa knew a Ragdoll's average lifespan was twelve to fifteen years, and now she feared her precious Sky was coming to the end of hers.

Lisa peeked at the fluffy, creamy beige-and-gray cat hiding between the back leg of the sofa and the side table. Sky's big blue eyes met hers.

"No need to move, girl," Lisa assured Sky. "If you're happy there, you stay there. You've earned some peace and quiet."

As Lisa began folding the blankets on the sofa, memories from long ago started playing through her mind:

The squeals of delight from her children, Emmy and Ryan, who had been just five and seven years old when she placed an eight-week-old Sky in their hands. The lights of the Christmas tree had paled in comparison to the joy on their faces that day.

Curtains curled up over the rod like ocean waves cresting in their family room so that a curious and determined Sky couldn't climb them.

A baby gate placed in the doorway to the enclosed porch after Sky shredded part of the screen.

Waking up to find Sky sleeping on Phil's chest, despite her husband claiming he had no affection for the cat.

Sky pawing the bay window every time a squirrel entered the backyard, meowing in chorus with the songbirds in the morning, and watching at the front window for Emmy and Ryan to return home from school.

Lisa sank into the sofa as she remembered sitting and crying with Sky on her children's beds after dropping each one off at college. Sky had seen every tear, heard every laugh, and been privy to every worry. Her willingness to be held provided soothing comfort to Lisa's heart.

"Oh, sweet girl," Lisa said. "What am I going to do without you? You've been such an important part of this family."

Sky crept from her hiding spot and silently walked to the back door. She peered through the closed glass door to the screened-in porch. The damage to the screen from Sky's sharp claws had taken so long to get repaired and the new furniture they put out there had been so expensive that Sky had been forbidden entrance ever since.

Lisa stood up and opened the door wide. An autumn breeze wafted through the opening. Sky stood rooted to the ground as if held back by an invisible barrier.

"It's okay, girl. It's high time you get your porch privileges back." Lisa crossed the threshold and went to her favorite glider.

Sky hesitated and then, as if testing the water, put one paw through the doorway. She took a first tentative step. A second one. She crept along the back wall of the porch and plopped beside a potted plant.

The phone rang, and Lisa went into the kitchen to answer the call. Her heart soared to hear Emmy's voice on the other end. Her daughter wanted to tell her all about the fall formal she had been invited to the night before. Mother and daughter chatted for quite a while before Emmy had to go. Lisa smiled as she hung up. Her once painfully shy little girl was growing into a confident and capable young woman.

Lisa returned to the porch, expecting to find Sky still hiding by the ficus. But instead, the Ragdoll was perched on the ottoman, looking out over the backyard.

Meow, she greeted Lisa.

Lisa smiled and sat in the chair next to the ottoman. Sky stood, stretched, and then climbed onto Lisa's lap and began purring loudly.

Lisa and Sky sat together for over an hour, both content, neither wanting to move. Eventually, when Lisa had to get back to her to-do list, she gently set Sky on the chair.

"It's all yours, girl. You enjoy this room and this furniture as much as you want."

And Sky did. For the next two years a happy, affectionate, and at times even playful cat spent every waking moment on that porch. A porch Lisa and Phil renamed Sky's room.

PAWS & PONDER...

How do you feel about getting older? What hard-won wisdom from life experiences could you share with someone today? How might a strong young person and an experienced older person bless each other? How could you bless someone today—either out of the strength of your youth or the experience of your age?

Paws & Pray

Lord, you are the God of all my days. Keep me focused on you in every season of life. Use me to help others around me. Teach me to use my strength, my experience, and the abilities you have given me to serve you, to respect others, and to love well.

HEARTFELT COUNSEL

The heartfelt counsel of a friend is as sweet as perfume and incense.

PROVERBS 27:9

A WAVE OF PANIC rushed over Cindy as she merged onto the interstate heading east out of Colorado—away from the state she had called home for seven years and the secure teaching job she had held since finishing grad school. *What am I doing?* she thought as she steered her small Mitsubishi Eclipse, packed full of boxes and suitcases, into the middle lane of traffic—squeezed between a large SUV and an even larger semitruck. *Is this a rash decision?*

Meeooww!

Cindy's one-year-old cat, Guinevere, had not stopped crying since being unceremoniously placed into a brand-new cat carrier and secured into the passenger seat.

"I know, sweetie. I know. This is scary for you," Cindy said, keeping her voice soothing. "For whatever it's worth, it's scary for me, too."

Still, Guinevere continued to cry, sounding more pitiful with each mile.

"I promise to let you out of this soon. Just let me get through Denver, okay?" Cindy placed her right hand against the front of the carrier. "Then it's wide-open road, and maybe you can come out."

The bumper-to-bumper traffic gave Cindy plenty of time to reflect out loud. She was glad that someone was there to listen.

"Gwen, I had a good job. Sure, I wasn't happy . . ." Guinevere responded with a low groan that gave Cindy pause. "Okay, okay, you're right. I was miserable. But it was a job with a steady paycheck. And I just walked away from it to pursue this crazy idea of getting into publishing. Who does that? And what if it doesn't work? What if this job at the newspaper isn't the step into publishing I think it could be? What if I end up being stuck as an entry-level beat reporter forever? What if I have to start sharing your Fancy Feast meals? What if . . ."

Wrraaoo.

Cindy was startled by the primal sound erupting from her cat and nearly swerved into the other lane. Gwen had never done that before. Once again, Cindy reached over and put her hand on the carrier to try to comfort her companion. As she glanced in the rearview mirror, she realized how far they had come.

"Well, look at that," she said in surprise. "We made it through Denver. Okay, Gwennie, I'm going to open the carrier. But don't freak me out. If you jump on the floor by my feet and the car pedals, we could get in an accident."

Guinevere shot out of the carrier the moment the latch was released and curled up in Cindy's lap. Cindy stroked her gently and continued to assure her trembling cat.

"Gwen, this is going to be an adventure for us. You're going to love the Midwest, I promise. It's where I grew up, and it's the best. You're going to be surrounded by so many people who love you."

Guinevere's trembling diminished to a slight quiver.

Cindy continued, "And wait till you see the colors in the fall. Yes, the aspens in Colorado are pretty, but where we're going the trees turn red, purple, orange, and yellow. It's incredible! And oh!" she shouted in excitement, causing Guinevere to jump. "Sorry, baby, but I just thought about your goopy eye. Remember how the vet said your eye would do better with more humidity? Well, guess what our destination has lots of? Humidity! I bet your eye is going to feel so much better!"

Cindy felt Guinevere calm down with a resonant purr.

"We are going to get to play together, and Mommy will pursue her dream job. Everything will work out."

Realistically, Cindy knew there would be difficult days ahead, and she still felt a little anxious about all the unknowns. But the more she talked to Guinevere, the more she began to believe her own words.

Fourteen hours later, Cindy pulled into her parents' driveway—exhausted from the long trip and yet at peace with her decision.

Holding Guinevere tightly in her arms, she walked to the front door. "No matter what the future holds, you and I are going to be just fine."

PAWS & PONDER...

Why do you think Cindy's anxieties about her move were eased the more she talked to Guinevere? To whom do you turn when you need to talk things over or receive heartfelt counsel? What is some of the best counsel or advice you have ever been given? What made that counsel "sweet as perfume and incense"?

_____   🐾   _____

Paws & Pray

Father, thank you for being my wonderful Counselor and for always being there for me. Thank you for the people you have placed in my life who speak loving truth to me. Please give me a passion for your Word so I can be a person who is willing and able to give wise and heartfelt counsel to others.

NICE TO MEET YOU

Rich and poor have this in common: The LORD is the Maker of them all.

PROVERBS 22:2, NIV

THE AIR WAS THICK with tension as two animals, vastly different in size and temperament, warily crept toward each other. Stopping three feet apart, they froze. Not a muscle twitch nor a flick of the tail could be detected.

The show-quality Irish setter named Fiona stared intently at the white cat recently dubbed Swiper.

"Mama, are they gonna be friends?" eight-year-old Marlee whispered.

"Shhh . . . ," her brother Max commanded.

"They'll be okay," Catherine spoke softly, hoping she was right. "We just need to let them say hello."

The family had been working toward this moment for weeks—ever since discovering the stray cat under the deck at the back of the house. Over time, as the cat began losing her fear of the humans who offered her food, she ventured closer and closer to their back door. That fact seemed to highly offend Fiona—who would bark viciously at the strange creature on the deck.

The kids didn't want to disturb the skittish cat, so they put Fiona on a leash and took her out through the front door whenever she needed to take care of business.

"Poor dog. She can't even run in her own yard anymore," Brian, Fiona's human dad, observed one evening. "I think it's time the animals meet so Fiona can have her yard back."

After much protesting, the family decided to intentionally have the two get acquainted.

But now, sensing the potential aggression building in her dog, Catherine was second-guessing the meet-and-greet.

If the cat runs off, the kids are going to be devastated, she thought.

Fiona remained tense, and Catherine kept a tight grip on the leash. Anticipating that Fiona might lunge, she was ready to pull the Irish setter back at any moment—when the cat casually walked over and rubbed her head against the dog's chest. As if in a trance, Fiona stood motionless, her head cocked to the side. The cat rubbed along Fiona's side. She brushed against Fiona's back legs. She even walked under the sixty-pound dog!

Catherine heard her daughter suck in a deep breath.

Apparently satisfied that Fiona meant her no harm, the cat curled up on the deck.

Released from the cat's mesmerizing power, Fiona bounded over to Swiper. She play-bowed and bumped her nose on the cat. She sniffed the stray's ears. And then, to the family's surprise, Fiona lay down right next to the cat.

"I don't believe it," Catherine whispered to her husband, who was looking very pleased with himself.

That day marked the beginning of a genuine friendship between the pampered pooch named Fiona and the stray named Swiper.

The two animals were as different as could be—from their size, to their species, to their temperaments. But somehow, someway, they became friends.

Friends who would call to each other from opposite sides of the back door.

Friends who would nuzzle each other and lie together in the sun.

Friends who would walk together in the evening with their human family—Fiona on a leash, Swiper running alongside.

And friends who were not the least bit concerned that people would say they weren't supposed to be.

Just two friends willing to take the time to get to know each other.

PAWS & PONDER...

Fiona and Swiper could not have been more different, and yet their differences are what made their friendship so special. In a world full of divisions—political, socioeconomic, spiritual—it is easy to forget that God is the Maker of us all. What differences are hard for you to see past in others? How do you think God wants his children to respond to those who are different from them?

Paws & Pray

Lord God, you made the world and filled it with people who are different from me in countless ways. God, help me to see others as you see them—fearfully and wonderfully created in your image. And when I become shortsighted and start to focus on the differences, convict me and remind me that you are the Maker and Creator of us all.

MUNCHKIN'S EXISTENTIAL CRISIS

A discerning person keeps wisdom in view,
but a fool's eyes wander to the ends of the earth.

PROVERBS 17:24, NIV

MUNCHKIN WAS ONE OF THE SMARTEST cats Cheri had ever known. Not only could he open drawers—a feat which both impressed and frustrated her—but Munchkin also seemed to have an awareness of the laws of physics, or at least how they applied to his favorite ping-pong ball. Munchkin carried the small plastic ball in his mouth everywhere. Several times throughout the day, he would drop his ball and amuse himself by batting it back and forth. Inevitably, however, the ball would roll under the sofa or the coffee table and get stuck, causing Munchkin to elicit a plaintive cry for help.

One day, Munchkin took his prized possession into the bathroom. Curious, Cheri followed him and was flabbergasted when she found her cat patting his ping-pong ball back and forth—in the bathtub. The high sides of the porcelain tub kept his ball safely contained, allowing him to play to his heart's content.

Months later, Munchkin confirmed his high intelligence when Cheri's other cat, Meeka, got stuck in a tree. While she and her husband stood debating how to get Meeka down, Munchkin shimmied up an adjacent tree, meowed, and began showing Meeka how to descend the tree, one branch at a time.

"You are one smart cat," Cheri praised him after both cats were safely on the ground.

And yet much like kryptonite to Superman, Munchkin's brilliance could not stand up to one powerful foe—the vastness of a high corner in Cheri and Daniel's apartment.

Having recently moved into a new apartment with limited space, Cheri and Daniel kept a tall stack of boxes—about six feet high—in the corner of the family room. The boxes were out of the way and yet accessible, ready for that day in the future when Cheri was sure she'd find time to go through them.

In the meantime, the different-sized boxes served as a jungle gym for Meeka, who enjoyed climbing them, jumping from them, and hiding things behind them. But for Munchkin, the boxes became a vertical pathway to a feline existential crisis.

Cheri would watch with befuddled amusement as her highly capable cat would excitedly climb to the top of the box tower. However, instead of turning around and perching on the heights to look down upon his kingdom, Munchkin would stare into the corner where the two white walls joined. After several minutes, he would let out a pitiful cry of despair.

The sound was mournful—almost as if he had given up all hope of ever being rescued. Mesmerized, Munchkin would repeat the sorrowful lament while leaning closer and closer toward the stark emptiness of the corner.

"It's like he has no idea he can just turn around and climb down," Cheri marveled the first time she witnessed the scene. She walked over to her forlorn cat and gently turned him around to face the room. It was a routine she would repeat countless times over the next several months.

And each time Munchkin would seem startled by his familiar surroundings. His head would shoot up, he would take two steps back, and bump into the corner that, moments before, had rendered him hopeless. He would then meow happily—a meow of victory before descending the box tower, retrieving his ping-pong ball from the floor, and scampering off to play some bathtub ball.

"Oh, Munchkin," Cheri said with a chuckle. "The trouble you could avoid if you'd keep your eye on the ball and off the wall."

PAWS & PONDER...

Munchkin was smart, but when he faced a certain wall, he would forget where he was and how to move forward. What are some "walls" that tend to get you stuck? How do you get turned around? What are some practical ways you can wisely avoid the distractions of this world?

Paws & Pray

Lord, I admit there have been times I've wandered away, become distracted, and forgotten what you've taught me. Please help me to focus on you and on your Word so I might avoid becoming stuck or trapped by the foolishness of this world. And when I do veer off course, take my hand and lead me on the right path that will bring me joy.

AN EXAMPLE FOR ROSIE

The fear of man lays a snare,
but whoever trusts in the LORD is safe.

PROVERBS 29:25, ESV

BETH USED TO WORRY that her cat Rosie was lonely without a feline sibling. Most of Beth's cat-loving friends had multiple feline pals who snuggled together, played together, and ate together—and apparently loved having their pictures taken doing all of the above. Rosie, on the other hand, detested sitting still for the camera and was perfectly content being a loner, which suited Beth, who also found social interactions somewhat taxing at times. It wasn't that she didn't like people; she had several close friends. But she often felt awkward around people she didn't know, and she normally found small talk and chitchat exhausting.

Beth much preferred her quiet nights at home with Rosie to nights out with her friends. Rosie was a comforting confidante, and Beth never worried about looking silly or saying the wrong thing to her.

But when the pandemic mandates shut down much of her surrounding area and brought an abrupt end to most social gatherings, Beth found herself missing the events she used to consider tedious. Day after day, she and Rosie went through their routine of eating meals, Rosie napping while Beth worked, and sitting on the sofa binging on Netflix.

Several weeks into the pandemic, Beth realized she missed getting calls from her friends to meet for a night out. She even wished she could go to a party or a live concert.

As weeks turned into months, Beth began to suspect that her previous distaste for social gatherings had less to do with a lack of interest and much more to do

with fear. And after living in what was starting to seem like a constant state of fear, Beth realized she was tired of being afraid.

It was time to stand up to her fears—or at least one of them.

Beth decided to take one small, courageous step. She could get to know her neighbors—something she had been avoiding since she moved into the neighborhood a year earlier.

Beth began by saying hello to the elderly man across the street when they both retrieved their mail. A few days later, she delivered a package to her next-door neighbor that had mistakenly been left by Beth's front door. She even spent several minutes talking with the neighbor about their mutual love of gardening. While they were conversing, the young boy who lived on the other side of Beth passed by on a scooter and waved. He was wearing a dragon costume that made Beth smile as she waved back.

Interacting with my neighbors isn't as intimidating as I thought, Beth mused. *It's actually kind of fun.*

Well, at least it was to her. Rosie, however, did not share Beth's new interest in their neighbors. In fact, the little cat—who usually enjoyed spending time outside—would dash inside the moment Beth waved at a neighbor.

"Come on, Rosie," Beth would encourage her. "If I can be friendly, you can be friendly."

Rosie flicked her tail in response and retreated into the house.

One day, the boy sporting the dragon costume was playing outside when he spotted Rosie resting on Beth's deck.

"You have a kitty!" the boy shouted, running into Beth's yard.

Rosie gave a questioning meow and looked wide-eyed at Beth.

"You're safe, Rosie," Beth assured her. "I'm right here. Go ahead and say hello to the little boy."

"I'm Alec," the boy said. "Can I say hi to your cat?"

Rosie looked at Beth, then at Alec, then back at Beth.

Beth held her breath. Would Rosie get spooked and run away?

"You can come over and say hi," Beth answered, willing Rosie to be brave.

After a moment of hesitation, Rosie rolled over and offered the little boy her belly. *Well, would you look at that,* Beth marveled.

Alec gave Rosie a gentle but thorough belly rub. "My friend Cameron has a cat. But I can't see Cameron right now cause of the panda-emic. I like your cat. Thanks! See ya."

Beth's heart swelled with sympathy for the boy. The isolation was hard enough for an introverted adult, but she couldn't imagine how hard it must be for a sociable child. She also couldn't believe how calm and outgoing Rosie had been with Alec.

"Well, look at you," Beth said as she hugged her. "You made a new friend."

Rosie and Beth spent the rest of the summer taking baby steps away from fear—and delighting in the new friends they made along the way.

PAWS & PONDER...

In what ways does trusting in God keep us safe? What is the difference between caution and fear? What do you think "the fear of man" is referring to in this Proverb? In what ways can fear become a snare? What fear do you need to entrust to God?

Paws & Pray

Lord, fear seems like such a natural response these days. Everywhere I look there is something to fear—illness, violence, evil, loss, failure, and even just the fear of letting others down. Yet, in your Word, you say to trust you and not be afraid. Help me believe that you are bigger than my fears and my insecurities. You are my ever-present help in times of trouble.

CAN'T WE ALL JUST GET ALONG?

When people's lives please the LORD,
even their enemies are at peace with them.

PROVERBS 16:7

"NO, MA'AM!" Christina yelled, as she walked into the family room. Their beagle, Angie, was biting the family cat, Callie. "We do not eat our friends!"

Christina tightly held Angie by the collar as Callie bolted down the hall. Angie lunged, clearly wanting to give chase.

"Oh no you don't, missy," Christina chastised. "You are going to leave that cat alone and be nice!"

Ever since the family had adopted the sweet-natured cat in need of a home, their beagle had become obsessed with getting rid of her. Angie barked at Callie, chased her, stole her food, grabbed her by the neck, and had recently begun chewing Callie's tail while the poor cat hissed and scratched in protest. Christina was done with Angie's behavior. Surely, a dog and a cat could share a home peacefully.

It was time to begin training Angie in earnest. Christina taught her the "leave it" command—which applied to the cat, her food, and the litter box. She also taught Angie to lie on a particular cushion in the family room on the opposite side of the room from the cat's bed. In addition to rewarding Angie when she responded to the new commands, Christina also gave her a piece of kibble every time the cat entered a room, training Angie to run to her human instead of the cat.

"Good girl, Angie!" Christina praised her dog one morning, several weeks into their new training. Angie had walked right by a sleeping Callie, without so much as a sniff in her direction. And the night before, when the family had piled on the sofa to watch a movie together, Angie had curled up with Christina's daughter, Lindsey, while Callie had snuggled with her sons, Evan and Sam.

After rewarding Angie for her good behavior, Christina walked into the kitchen to pour herself a cup of French roast coffee, relishing a few tranquil moments. She inhaled the aroma of her coffee and soaked in the peaceful morning.

"Mom!" Lindsey shouted from upstairs. "Evan won't get out of the bathroom, and I *have* to get ready!"

Christina heard her daughter pounding on the door.

"I'm not done! Hold your horses!" Evan yelled through the door.

More pounding.

Christina smiled at Angie and Callie, now lying next to each other and looking perfectly content.

Wonder if treats would work with my kids too? she thought with a sigh.

PAWS & PONDER...

Living peacefully with Callie did not come naturally for Angie, the beagle. It required training. How might this truth apply to your life? How can you train yourself to better hear God's voice and obey his commands? Is there someone you are struggling to get along with? Ask for God's help to find a peaceful solution.

Paws & Pray

Lord, train me to hear your voice and obey your commands. I realize that humility and sacrifice are essential qualities for living a life of peace, but they do not come naturally to me. Help me live in a way that pleases you. Let your peace fill me and then be extended to those around me.

48

PANDA'S FAVORITE NAPPING SPOT

I am teaching you today—yes, you—so you will trust in the LORD.

PROVERBS 22:19

BROOKLYN'S CAT PANDA had always loved a good nap. The black-and-white cat could nap anywhere, and often did. Thankfully, living on Brooklyn's farm provided a variety of available places to snooze—from hay lofts to blueberry bushes, to tractors and overturned buckets. One of Panda's favorite napping places was on the blankets Brooklyn wrapped around the horses when the temperature dipped below freezing. During the warmer months, she stored the blankets in the feed room. Oftentimes when Brooklyn went inside the feed room, Panda followed her, curled up on one of the blankets, and fell asleep. One day, Brooklyn accidentally locked Panda in the small room, so she wisely taped a note on the door: *Check for Panda*.

Next to napping—and eating—Panda's other favorite pastime was watching visitors learn to ride the horses on the equine therapy farm. As a young kitten, Panda often ran away and hid when visitors arrived, unlike her feline brother and sister who would welcome guests. But over time, Panda learned that the visitors meant her no harm. They often just wanted to pet her—or even better, give her treats. Eventually Panda began looking for them at the round pen where children and adults groomed and rode the horses.

Sometimes Panda watched from the top of a nearby picnic table. But other times she would slip into the round pen, climb onto the mounting block, and watch the horses with the visitors on their backs. Several times, Brooklyn observed Panda leaning toward the horse and rider, as if she were studying their form and technique.

One bitterly cold winter day, Brooklyn was refilling the horses' water trough when she noticed Panda walking along the top of the fence. Her balance never ceased to amaze Brooklyn. But she could never have imagined her surefooted cat's next move.

PD, Brooklyn's oldest and most gentle gelding, was standing next to the fence, patiently awaiting a drink of fresh water. The weather report called for possible freezing drizzle overnight, so Brooklyn had wrapped all the horses in their blankets. PD looked particularly handsome in his dark navy-blue coat. As the quarter horse stood with his back end pressed against the fence, Panda extended one front leg toward the horse and touched his blanket. PD didn't flinch. Panda extended her other front leg and placed it on the blanket.

Brooklyn froze, the hose dangling from her hand, as Panda slowly moved her back legs onto PD and lay down on her favorite napping blanket.

"Oh boy . . ." Brooklyn whispered, unsure of how this was going to end.

Panda's head shot up as PD moved toward the water trough. Her front claws dug into the blanket. As soon as PD stopped, Panda flung herself at the fence, catching herself with her front legs and swinging for a moment before her back legs could grab on.

Grateful the unintended ride had ended without incident, Brooklyn went back to her chores. She assumed Panda would think twice about napping on a horse again.

But she was wrong.

Panda took advantage of the comfortable spot any time it was available. Over the course of the winter, whenever Panda found PD wearing his blanket and standing next to the fence, she would climb on his back. And the more times she climbed aboard, the more she got used to his movement. By the end of the winter, it wasn't unusual for Brooklyn to find Panda asleep on PD's back while the horse slowly made his way around the field.

A sleeping cat. A gentle horse. A beautiful picture of trust.

PAWS & PONDER...

Does trust come easily for you? Why or why not? How is trust earned? Do you believe that God is trustworthy? What are some ways he has proven his trustworthiness to you? What do you need to trust him with today?

_____   🐾   _____

Paws & Pray

God, I know that you are trustworthy, and yet so often I allow past hurts, doubt, and cynicism to override my trust in you. Retrain me to rely on you. To trust your will, your way, and your timing. Thank you for being a steady, faithful, and compassionate companion.

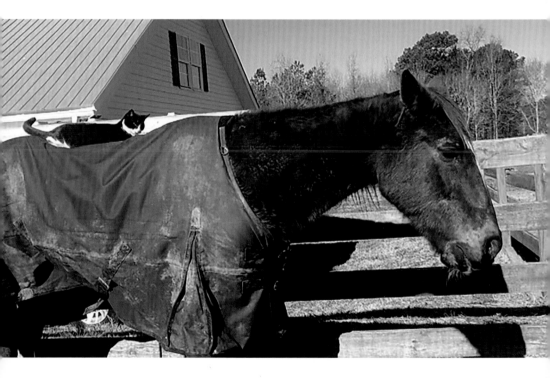

YOUR CAT NEEDS HELP

Listen to advice and accept instruction,
that you may gain wisdom in the future.

PROVERBS 19:20, ESV

KAREN AND ED were looking forward to visiting her family for the holidays, especially since they had a big announcement. Karen and Ed were expecting a baby. But before they could set off for Florida, they had to find a pet sitter for their cat, Abby.

The couple first saw Abby several months earlier during an adoption event at their local mall. The organizers told Karen and Ed that Abby was between two and three years of age. Her owner had been a man who traveled often and was no longer able to care for her. Karen and Ed immediately fell in love with her and were excited to experience the joy of being first-time pet parents. However, soon after bringing her home, Abby snuck up behind Karen and pounced on her, causing that joy to diminish a little.

Abby was affectionate and playful with Ed, but she would sporadically stalk and pounce on Karen.

"Maybe it's just going to take her a while to get used to a woman," Ed offered one night after intercepting Abby, who was making her way toward Karen. "After all, she lived with a workaholic bachelor for the first few years of her life. She's probably not used to women."

Karen hoped he was right.

And over the next several months, as Abby's surprise pounces all but disappeared, it appeared as though she was. Which was why they felt comfortable hiring a pet sitter for Abby so they could fly down to Florida and deliver their

news to Karen's parents in person. Arrangements were made for the sitter to come to the house twice a day to feed and care for Abby.

But just two days into their trip, Karen received a phone call from the sitter.

"I quit," she shouted into the phone. "That cat of yours needs help! She tries to attack me every time I come into the house."

"Uh-oh," Karen mouthed to Ed.

After confirming that Abby had not hurt the pet sitter at all, Karen and Ed, along with Karen's parents, scrambled to find other arrangements for Abby. Finally a neighbor agreed to put down food and fresh water each day but made it clear she would not linger in the house. Thankfully, there were no more phone calls about Abby.

Still, as the months went by, and the baby Karen was carrying grew more each passing day, Karen's worries about Abby and their soon-to-be-born child grew too. Karen knew they had to do something before the baby arrived.

"Surely there has to be a way to help her adjust to new people in the house, right?" Karen lamented to Ed one night. "I don't want to have to find a new place for her to live, but we have to protect this baby," she said, cradling her tummy.

The next day they took Abby to the vet.

"There's nothing physically wrong with Abby," the vet concluded after a thorough examination and several tests. "But I would like to refer Abby to a cat psychologist."

Karen and Ed had to keep from laughing out loud.

A cat psychologist?

Karen felt a bit ridiculous when she called to make an appointment with the *cat shrink*, as Ed called her. But they desperately wanted to keep Abby after the baby was born.

The next week the cat psychologist, Dr. Lloyd, came to the house to evaluate Abby in her natural environment. She asked many questions; observed Abby's interactions with Karen and Ed; studied Abby while she ate and when she rested; and interacted with Abby, in what Karen deduced were feline psychological tests. At the end of their almost two-hour-long visit, Dr. Lloyd diagnosed Abby with high anxiety and recommended several strategies from diet changes to behavior modifications to help lessen her symptoms.

"And as far as the new baby goes, try to prepare the house as much as possible as it will be when the baby arrives," Dr. Lloyd suggested. "Specifically, get the baby's room and crib all set up so that nothing will come as a surprise to Abby."

Karen and Ed took the cat psychologist's advice and even went so far as to get a doll which they wrapped in a blanket and kept in the crib. Sometimes Karen would carry the doll around with her, sing to it, and even put it in the baby swing.

"I feel ridiculous," she would occasionally complain to Ed.

But when their daughter was born, and Abby accepted her as if she'd always been there, Karen was glad she had followed the psychologist's advice. And since they were planning on adding another child to their family in the near future, Karen had no doubt she would be singing to the doll again soon.

PAWS & PONDER...

Why is it difficult sometimes to take instruction or advice from others? What is some advice you were glad you heeded? How can good advice and instruction help you gain wisdom in the future?

_____ 🐾 _____

Paws & Pray

God, thank you for your instruction. Soften my heart so that I will be willing to accept advice and direction from people who desire my good. Please give me wisdom, discernment, and courage so that I will know when and how to offer godly counsel to others.

UNLIKELY FRIENDS

A friend is always loyal, and a brother is born to help in time of need.

PROVERBS 17:17

CAROL AND SARAH weren't always friends.

It wasn't that they were enemies, but the women weren't what anyone would call close. They worked at the same company and they often were competing for the same projects. When the company restructured and merged Carol's and Sarah's separate divisions into one, the two suddenly found themselves having to work together toward a common goal. But trust didn't come easily, and interactions often were strained.

However, all of that began to change one day when the women arrived for a meeting a few minutes early and found themselves alone in the room.

Carol looked at the clock, hoping someone else would show up. And then . . .

"So, um, I hear you have a cat?" Sarah's question broke the awkward silence.

"Not a cat," Carol corrected Sarah. "THE cat. She is the single most wonderful, most beautiful kitten in the world." Carol braced herself for Sarah's reaction.

"What's her name?"

"Persephone."

Carol knew many people thought her devotion to Sephy—the nickname she often used for her—was over the top, but Carol didn't care. She loved Sephy and would gladly tell anyone who asked.

Sarah's smile expressed complete understanding.

"I have a dog. His name is Bullet, but we call him Bully. He is, by far, the greatest dog to have ever graced this planet. Want to see a picture of him?"

Carol nodded. Sarah scooted beside her and began scrolling through pictures on her phone. She talked about the dog she and her husband, Kory, had rescued

several years earlier with the same passion and affection that Carol used when talking about Sephy. Soon, Carol was scrolling through her own phone. The two women were laughing at and admiring the pictures.

When others began to filter into the room, the phones were tucked away, but the connection was just beginning.

Later that evening, Carol related what happened to her small companion. "Seph, I made a new friend today," Carol said. "And it was all because of you."

That same night, Sarah was having a similar conversation with Bully.

The tenseness between the two women slowly began to dissipate in the office. After a few weeks, Carol and Sarah were texting about a work project when Carol asked what Bully was doing.

Sarah texted a photo of Bully sleeping beside her.

Carol texted back one of Sephy, doing exactly the same thing.

From that moment, an endless thread of shared photos, videos, and memes began between the two women. Eventually, the text threads led to FaceTime videos. Carol and Sarah angled their cameras so that Bully and Sephy could see each other. As much as they wanted to make these in-person visits, Sarah was severely allergic to cats and Sephy was terrified of large animals. Video visits were the safest way to connect. But the friends (with the help of their human companions) didn't stop there.

Sephy and Bully received Secret Santa gifts from each other, Valentine's Day cards, photos to decorate the refrigerators in their kitchens, and treats just to say "I'm thinking of you." Carol was Sephy's personal shopper who gladly dug through a bin of pig's ears at the pet store to find the flat ones Bully preferred. Sarah, Bully's proxy, left thank-you cat treats and toys for Sephy on Carol's desk.

If Bully got sick or had a bad day, or Sephy had a scary run-in with a neighborhood dog or had a vet appointment, their humans would overnight care packages addressed to Bully or Persephone.

Even though the cat and dog had never actually met, Sephy and Bully's long-distance relationship was becoming an example of true love.

As for Carol and Sarah, they became "fill-ins" for their companions, via regular "Can I please come over and play with Bully or Sephy" visits.

Carol pops over to Sarah's house to accompany them on a walk, rub Bully's silky-soft ears, and watch Sarah prepare Bully's favorite treat—a piece of American cheese slathered in peanut butter that is then wrapped around a Beggin' Strip. (Carol calls it a Bullito.) Sarah's visits require a bit more planning. Carol vacuums for an hour and thoroughly cleans the house while Sarah takes a large dose of allergy medicine, and Sephy tries very hard to stay off the special chair designated for Ms. Sarah. But neither Carol nor Sarah mind the extra effort. To them, their visits are a chance to spend time celebrating and adoring the animals they bonded over.

Two unlikely friends who brought together two unlikely friends. One duo who have never met in person but who somehow manage to make each other's lives even richer. And the other who have become the best of friends—thanks to a sweet little kitty named Sephy and a wonderful hound named Bully.

PAWS & PONDER...

Who comes to mind when you read Proverbs 17:17? When have you needed a loyal friend to stand with you? Did they? How did they demonstrate their loyalty? How have you demonstrated your loyalty to a friend in a need?

——————————————— ❀ ———————————————

Paws & Pray

Lord, thank you for the gift of friendship and for the special friends you have given me. Please help me to extend grace, compassion, and kindness to them. Inspire me to make unlikely friendships and spread your love to those who need it.

ABOUT THE AUTHOR

JENNIFER MARSHALL BLEAKLEY is also the author of *Joey: How a Blind Rescue Horse Helped Others Learn to See* and *Project Solomon: The True Story of a Lonely Horse Who Found a Home—and Became a Hero*, as well as the Pawverbs devotional series. She has worked as a child and family grief counselor and holds a master's degree in mental health counseling from Nova Southeastern University. She lives in Raleigh, North Carolina, with her husband, Darrell, their two children, and a menagerie of animals. You can connect with Jen online at jenniferbleakley.com or on social media @jenbleakley.

ACKNOWLEDGMENTS

A **SPECIAL THANKS TO EVERYONE** whose cats inspired many of the stories in this book:

Carol Traver, Kory Atkinson, Madeline Daniels, Cheri Gregory, Amy Carroll, Dave Schroeder, Kim Miller, Trudy Miller, Kathy Quance, Brooklyn Stephens, Julie Gardner, Aimee Caverly, Patty Nagy, Judy Marshall, Jodi Grubbs, Nancy Marshall, Karen Vitantonio, and Andrew and Ella Bleakley. Thank you for sharing your stories and your beloved cats with me.

To Sarah Atkinson, Bonne Steffen, Carol Traver, Ron Kaufmann, and the amazing team at Tyndale House, thank you so much for your work on this project. It is an honor and a joy to work on these books with you. Thank you for sharing your stories with me; for making these books look so beautiful; and for allowing me to talk and write about animals all day long—and get to call it work!

Darrell, Andrew, Ella, Mom, Dad, Aunt Judy, and my precious friends who pray for me and encourage me during the writing process, thank you for always being there, for encouraging me in so many ways, and for always pointing me to the One who is able to do immeasurably more than I could ever ask or imagine. I am so grateful for you.

Lord, thank you for the gift of animals and for all the ways you speak to us and touch our hearts through them.

And lastly, I'd like to acknowledge three very special animals:

Persephone, I don't know if there has ever been a kitty more loved than you. Thank you for providing such inspiration for this book and for being such a talented, accomplished, and wonderful kitty for your mom.

Bullet, there is a good reason your mom bought you a cape—you, sweet boy, are a true superhero! You have brought so much joy to so many people—your mom most of all. Thank you for being such a big part of the Pawverbs family. And thank you for loving your mom so well.

And to my sweet and feisty Foxy, thank you for choosing us all those years ago. And thank you for providing such inspiration while I wrote this book. I couldn't have done it without you laying across my keyboard, sticking your head in my coffee, or swatting at my hands as I typed. My life is richer and far more fun with you in it.

PHOTOGRAPHY CREDITS

Unless otherwise noted, interior photographs are from Shutterstock and are the property of their respective copyright holders, and all rights are reserved. Listed by page number:

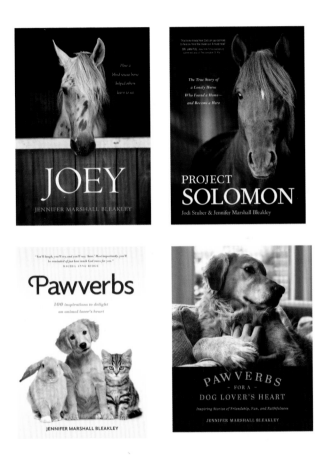

Available everywhere
books are sold.